Samina Iqbal is a senior public law and immigration practitioner with over 20 years' experience and the joint-head of the immigration and public law team in Chambers. Given her expertise in immigration, nationality and asylum law, she has been ranked as a Leading Junior in Legal 500 (Tier 3), as well as, Chambers & Partners (Tier 4). More recently, Samina's growing specialism has been in challenges to unlawful detention, crossing over with claims for damages in the civil courts. Her expertise and vast experience in this area means she is often considered by her instructing solicitors as the "go-to" person for such cases. She has also delivered extensive training seminars and webinars in this areas of the law.

She is a versatile lawyer, dynamic and fair, relentless in her pursuit of a positive resolutions for her clients. Also instructed in SIAC work and a recognised immigration expert in family proceedings. Samina's expertise in this area is underlined by the article she co-authored in the IANLJ, Family and Immigration Proceedings – treading the minefield for the practitioner".

Samina is committed to levelling the playing field throughout all echelons of our society, expanding her practice to include those who require assistance in community care law, equality and discrimination law, social welfare, mental health and capacity law.

Samina was also first appointed as a fee-paid First-Tier Tribunal Judge of the Immigration and Asylum Chamber in 2006 and subsequently to the Social Entitlement Chamber in 2018 and as an Environment and Traffic Adjudicator in 2017.

She is committed to inspiring and training more junior women at the Bar, being acutely aware of gender disparities in the profession and has been recognised for her selfless social activism and dedication; as 'Champion of the Year' for Inspirational Women in Law Awards 2020 and nominated as 'International Pro Bono Barrister of the Year' in the Advocate Bar Pro Bono Awards 2[illegible]

A Practical Guide to Claims for Unlawful Detention and False Imprisonment in Immigration and Asylum Cases

A Practical Guide to Claims for Unlawful Detention and False Imprisonment in Immigration and Asylum Cases

Samina Iqbal
Barrister, Lincolns Inn
LLB (Hons)

Law Brief Publishing

The information in this book was believed to be correct at the time of writing. All content is for information purposes only and is not intended as legal advice. No liability is accepted by either the publisher or author for any errors or omissions (whether negligent or not) that it may contain. Professional advice should always be obtained before applying any information to particular circumstances.

Published 2020 by Law Brief Publishing, an imprint of Law Brief Publishing Ltd
30 The Parks
Minehead
Somerset
TA24 8BT

www.lawbriefpublishing.com

Paperback: 978-1-912687-97-8

For my father

CONTENTS

OVERVIEW

The terms "unlawful detention" and "false imprisonment" are often used interchangeably. Unlawful detention is commonly used to determine, in the context of immigration cases, whether the Secretary of State has acted without valid legal authority to detain an individual. However, false imprisonment refers to a situation under common law, which gives rise to a civil claim for damages. It is a strict liability tort and no demonstrable loss is needed to establish this. For the purposes of this guide the term unlawful detention will be used more generally.

In the first instance an individual's detention will be considered against the statutory power under which they have been detained. Therefore, the first question will always be whether, in law, there is a power to detain an individual. If the answer to this question is in the affirmative, which more often than not will be the case, then the next step would be to go on to consider the following matters in relation to the detention:

- Can the individual apply for immigration bail? There is a separate chapter (chapter 5) that deals specifically with immigration bail, the current regime and the basis on which the release from detention can be sought. However, it must be kept in mind that there will be no assessment at this stage, as to whether the detention itself is unlawful.

If an individual were not entitled to bail or bail was refused, the next steps in relation to detention, would be to consider whether:

- The detention was in breach of the '*Hardial Singh*' principles? and/or;

- There was a failure to apply the relevant detention policies of the Secretary of State for the Home Department which are material to the decision to detain, such that it amounts to a public law error? and/or;

- Whether the detention itself was in breach of the European Convention on Human Rights, in particular Article 5 and the right to liberty and security?

If there are suspicions of detention not being in accordance with statutory powers, policies and/or principles then the challenge can be brought by way of judicial review on grounds that should be identified after a full factual assessment of a detainee's immigration history, for periods of detention that may be considered unlawful.

Although not so common, if an individual alleges that there has been no power to detain them, then they may look at the remedy of issuing an application for a writ of Habeas Corpus against the Secretary of State for the Home Department, which would require them to produce the individual at court and to prove that they were lawfully detained.

In any claim for judicial review, there may be an additional claim for damages in relation to any period of detention claimed to be unlawful. If a finding is made by the high court that detention was unlawful then determination of the quantum would be transferred to the Queen's Bench Division (QBD) or county courts for them to determine. Separate to this there may be someone who simply seeks damages for a historic period of detention, in which case they will have to look to the civil courts applying the same principles of law, when attempting to demonstrate the period of detention that is unlawful.

Assessing the level of damages will always be quite tricky, one often wants to find a quick answer to the question of "is this period of immigration detention unlawful?" in particular in relation to claim for damages. However, it is necessary to make an assessment using the relevant principles to work out whether an individual will be entitled to damages. There is a dedicated chapter on damages (chapter 8) in this guide to ensure an understanding of whether an individual ought to pursue a claim, having made such an assessment, especially where it has been established, for example, that only an award for "nominal damages" was likely.

This guide does not intend to comprehensively cover all aspects of unlawful detention but seeks to enable anyone starting out in this area to do so with some confidence. The law restated in this guide is as it stands at 1st October 2020. At the time of writing there have recently been exciting developments in relation to immigration detention, with the House of Lords voting to amend the new Immigration Bill to include a statutory 28 day limit. This will certainly be a welcome addition to the law limiting detention.

CHAPTER ONE
STATUTORY FRAMEWORK ON DETENTION

Introduction

In order to live and work in the UK, individuals who are not British citizens must have a lawful basis[1] on which they have been permitted to stay and at the same time not be in breach of any immigration laws.

The Home Office have the power granted by Parliament under various legislation to detain anyone for the purposes of immigration control. The reasons for detention are generally to effect an individual's removal and/or deportation, although there are a host of other reasons for detention, for example to establish a person's identity or where there is reason to believe that the person will fail to comply with any conditions attached if they were released.

There are also certain situations in which British citizens may be detained but that is currently beyond the scope of this guide.[2]

---

1 This refers to those who are foreign nationals including, EU nationals and/or their family member with relevant leave to remain, have been granted indefinite leave to remain or have limited leave to remain (based on work, study or family/private life) as well as those without leave.

2 The case of *Home Office v TR & Anor* [2019] EWHC 49 (QB) is worth reading in this context.

Statutory Powers and Home Office Policy

It is important to consider the legal safeguards which ensure when an individual is deprived of their liberty it is done by reference to the relevant statutory framework and in accordance within the Home Office policy on detention. In addition, detention must also be guided by the restrictions suggested by domestic and ECHR case law.

Therefore the first step in considering any claim for unlawful detention is to consider the legislative powers under which an individual is being held. The relevant legislation on detention can be found in the following four Acts:

- Immigration Act 1971 ("1971 Act");
- Immigration and Asylum Act 1999 ("1999 Act");
- Nationality, Immigration and Asylum Act 2002 ("2002 Act"); and
- UK Borders Act 2007 ("2007 Act")

(i) Immigration Act 1971 (as amended by the 1999 Act)

The Home Office powers of arrest and detention come largely from the 1971 Act and in particular, paragraph 16 of Schedule 2 to the 1971 Act (as applied by section 10 (7) of the Immigration and Asylum Act 1999 and section 62 of the Nationality, immigration and Asylum Act 2002 (see below)) which, provides for the detention of illegal entrants and overstayers liable to examination or removal in the following terms:

- Schedule 2, Paragraph 16 (1) states: *"A person who may be required to submit to examination under paragraph 2 above may be detained under the authority of an immigration officer pending his examination and pending a decision to give or refuse him leave to enter."*

- Schedule 2, Paragraph 16 (1A) states: *"A person whose leave to enter has been suspended under paragraph 2A may be detained under the authority of an immigration officer pending—(a)completion of his examination under that paragraph; and (b)a decision on whether to cancel his leave to enter."*

- Schedule 2, Paragraph 16 (2) states: *If there are reasonable grounds for suspecting that a person is someone in respect of whom directions may be given under any of paragraphs 8 to 10A or 12 to 14, that person may be detained under the authority of an immigration officer pending— (a) a decision whether or not to give such directions; (b) his removal in pursuance of such directions*

(ii) UK Borders Act 2007

Where an individual is subject to deportation action or a deportation order is in force against an individual, the Secretary of State has the power to detain, as set out in paragraph 2 of Schedule 3 to the 1971 Act and section 36 of the 2007 Act (governing automatic deportation):

- Schedule 3, Paragraph 2 (1) states: " *Where a recommendation for deportation made by a court is in force in respect of any person, and that person is not detained in pursuance of the sentence or order of any court, he shall... be detained pending the making of a deportation order in pursuance of the recommendation, unless—(a)the court by which the recommendation is made grants bail to the person, or (b)the person is released on immigration bail under Schedule 10 to the Immigration Act 2016."*

- Schedule 3, Paragraph 2 (2) states "*Where notice has been given to a person in accordance with regulations under section 105 of the Nationality, Immigration and Asylum Act 2002 (notice of decision) of a decision to make a deportation order against him, and he is not detained in pursuance of the sentence or order of a court, he may be detained under the authority of the Secretary of State pending the making of the deportation order."*

- Schedule 3, Paragraph 2 (3) states "*Where a deportation order is in force against any person, he may be detained under the authority of the Secretary of State pending his removal or departure from the United Kingdom (and if already detained by virtue of sub-paragraph (1) or (2) above when the order is made, shall continue to be detained unless he is released on immigration bail under Schedule 10 to the Immigration Act 2016"*

The 2007 Act also contains provisions for detention under section 36. This considers detention of those who may be subject to automatic detention following a period of imprisonment of a minimum period of 12 months, in the following terms:

"(1) A person who has served a period of imprisonment may be detained under the authority of the Secretary of State–

(a) while the Secretary of State considers whether section 32(5) [on automatic deportation] applies, and

(b) where the Secretary of State thinks that section 32(5) applies, pending the making of the deportation order."

(iii) Nationality, Immigration and Asylum Act 2002

A more recent extension to the Secretary of State's power to detain (separate to the authorisation given to immigration officers by the 1971 Act) comes from section 62 of the Nationality, Immigration and Asylum Act 2002. This is a stand-alone provision that allows detention in cases where the Secretary of State has the power to set removal directions.

(iv) Home Office Policies

As already highlighted above, there are also a number of Home Office Policies, which provide a comprehensive overview of how in practice, the legislation ought to be applied. These will be considered in below in chapter 3. Whilst, policy is not considered to have the same status as statute[3], the guidance it provides must certainly be considered before detention is authorised or indeed is maintained. The three most relevant policies (found on the gov.uk website under Guidance on immigration offender management for officers dealing with enforcement immigration matters within the UK)[4] are:

---

3 *Alvi [2012] UKSC 33* which endorsed the Court of Appeal's decision in *Secretary of State for the Home Department v Pankina [2010] EWCA Civ 719* also see *Pokhriyal* [2013] EWCA Civ 1568 [42-43] and *Lumba* [2011] UKSC 12 [35] and to similar effect *Mandalia* [2015] UKSC 59 [29]-[31]),

4 https://www.gov.uk/government/publications/offender-management

- Chapter 55 – Detention and temporary release (formerly) Enforcement Instructions and Guidance[5] which is still relevant to historical claims for false imprisonment

- Chapter 55a – Detention of Pregnant Women dated 12th July 2016[6]

- Adult at risk in immigration Detention dated 6th March 2019[7] (also referred to as AAR policy)

5 https://assets.publishing.service.gov.uk/government/uploads/system/uploads/attachment_data/file/804785/Chapter-55-detention-v26.0ext.pdf

6 https://assets.publishing.service.gov.uk/government/uploads/system/uploads/attachment_data/file/653012/Chapter_55a_Detention_of_pregnant_women_v1.pdf

7 https://assets.publishing.service.gov.uk/government/uploads/system/uploads/attachment_data/file/784634/adults-at-risk-policy-v5.0ext.pdf

CHAPTER TWO
LIMITS ON DETENTION

GENERAL PRINCIPLES – LIMITS ON DETENTION

It has often been noted that the UK is the only country in the EU with no time limit on detention[1]. However, Woolf J (as he was then and later the Lord Chief Justice)in the case of ***R v Governor of Durham Prison ex parte Hardial Singh*** [1984] 1 WLR 704, explored the power to detain for immigration purposes and gave guidance, emphasising the importance for limitations on detention. These principles developed under common law are now known as the '*Hardial Singh*' principles. Whilst, these principles are based on public law errors they can be distinguished as discrete principles in law, developed through case law, with which detention must comply.

The 'Hardial Singh' principles have been endorsed time and again with the European Courts of Human Rights concluding that the Hardial Singh principles ensured checks were in place, the UK detention system which, did not breach Article 5 of the ECHR[2].

1 The UK has opted out of the Directive 2008/115/EC on common standards and procedures in Member States for returning illegally staying third-country nationals ("the Returns Directive"), which does set out at Article 15 of Chapter IV, a maximum time limit of 18 months for detention pending deportation.

2 Article 5 *(1) Everyone has the right to liberty and security of person. No one shall be deprived of his liberty save in the following cases and in accordance with a procedure prescribed by law:*
(a) the lawful detention of a person after conviction by a competent court
(b) the lawful arrest or detention of a person for non-compliance with the lawful order of a court or in order to secure the fulfilment of any obligation prescribed by law
(c) the lawful arrest or detention of a person effected for the purpose of bringing him before the competent legal authority on reasonable suspicion of having committed an offence or when it is reasonably considered necessary to prevent his committing an offence or fleeing after having done so

However this does not mean that individuals would never be able to demonstrate a violation of their Article 5 rights.

More recently, in the case of ***J.N. v. the United Kingdom*, Application no. 37289/12, 19 May 2016**[3] the European Courts of Human Rights again rejected the proposition that the system of immigration detention in the United Kingdom fell short of the requirements of Article 5(1)(f). The courts had previously considered and rejected the complaint in the context of the UK's lack of time-limits, in the cases of ***Abdi v. the United Kingdom, no. 27770/08, 9 April 2013 and Saadi v. the United Kingdom, no. 13229/03***. In any case, it was held that simply because a country did have time-limits prescribed under domestic law, did not mean an automatic conformity would be assumed with the protections of Article 5(1)(f).[4]

(d) the detention of a minor by lawful order for the purpose of educational supervision or his lawful detention for the purpose of bringing him before the competent legal authority

(e) the lawful detention of persons for the prevention of the spreading of infectious diseases, of persons of unsound mind, alcoholics or drug addicts or vagrants

(f) the lawful arrest or detention of a person to prevent his effecting an unauthorised entry into the country or of a person against whom action is being taken with a view to deportation or extradition.

(2) Everyone who is arrested shall be informed promptly, in a language which he understands, of the reasons for his arrest and of any charge against him.

(3) Everyone arrested or detained in accordance with the provisions of paragraph 1(c) of this Article shall be brought promptly before a judge or other officer authorised by law to exercise judicial power and shall be entitled to trial within a reasonable time or to release pending trial. Release may be conditioned by guarantees to appear for trial.

(4) Everyone who is deprived of his liberty by arrest or detention shall be entitled to take proceedings by which the lawfulness of his detention shall be decided speedily by a court and his release ordered if the detention is not lawful.

(5) Everyone who has been the victim of arrest or detention in contravention of the provisions of this Article shall have an enforceable right to compensation.

3 ***J.N. v. the United Kingdom*, Application no. 37289/12, 19 May 2016** – https://hudoc.echr.coe.int/eng#{"itemid":["001-162855"]}

4 §83 ibid

On the facts of ***J.N.*** however, a breach of Article 5(1)(f) was established as the Courts concurred with the Administrative Court's findings that the Secretary of State had shown, *"woeful lack of energy and impetus"* as the Applicant's deportation had not been pursued with "*due diligence*". The Applicant was an Iranian National who refused to cooperate with documentation procedures for removal, the Secretary of State contemplated prosecution under section 35 of the Asylum and Immigration (Treatment of Claimants, etc.) Act 2004, but took no further action. His repeated refusal to cooperate could not be considered a "*trump card*" to justify lengthy periods of detention which were no longer for the purpose of deportation. However, in assessing the factual background of the case the European Courts of Human Rights were more generous than the Administrative Court finding (under Hardial Singh – principle 4), that the period of unlawful detention was greater than what had been accepted and therefore confirmed that there was a breach of Article 5 (1)(f)[5].

This case gives clear guidance from the European Courts of Human Rights that the common law principles developed in the UK are sufficient in protecting individuals in detention cases and that even with the protection a time-limit, detention may still be unlawful.

5 §107 ibid

i *'Hardial Singh'* Principles

The *'Hardial Singh'* principles themselves can be summarised as outlined by Dyson LJ in ***I (Afghanistan)*** [2002] **EWCA Civ 888**[6] as follows:

i. The Secretary of State must intend to deport the person and can only use the power to detain for that purpose;

ii. The deportee may only be detained for a period that is reasonable in all the circumstances;

iii. If, before the expiry of the reasonable period, it becomes apparent that the Secretary of State will not be able to effect deportation within that reasonable period, he should not seek to exercise the power of detention;

iv. The Secretary of State should act with reasonable diligence and expedition to effect removal.

The Supreme Court in ***R (Lumba & Mighty) v Secretary of State for the Home Department [2011] UKSC 12*** and in the case heard immediately after that of ***SK (Zimbabwe) v Secretary of State for the Home Department [2011] UKSC 23*** further endorsed and refined the formulation of the *'Hardial Singh'* Principles. Whilst, both cases concluded that a failure to apply a relevant policy in reviewing detention, would render detention unlawful, it was found that this in itself this could only lead to nominal damages as the detainees would have been detained any way. However, if they were able to demonstrate that detention would not have be justified on *'Hardial Singh'* principles, then this could lead potentially to a greater award in damages.

---

6 §48 of *I (Afghanistan)* [2002] EWCA Civ 888)

Hardial Singh Principles 1 – Power to Detain

A breach of this principle is very rare and not commonly seen in practice as the Home Office/Secretary of State, will inevitably use their statutory powers identified to lawfully justify detention, the focus will therefore be on the other '*Hardial Singh*' principles, where the courts have found most unlawful detention cases to fall.

Hardial Singh Principles 2 and 3 – Reasonable Period

Both these principles two and three are interlinked and when examining if detention was for a reasonable period in the second principle, it inevitably leads to consideration of the third principle in relation whether at the end of that reasonable period, removal would be effective.

In order to assess what would be considered a "*reasonable period*" it is important to consider the guidance of Lord Dyson in ***Lumba,*** who listed a number of factors (previously considered in his judgment of ***I (Afghanistan)*** **[2002] EWCA Civ 888**[7]. He highlighted the following matters as relevant:

- the length/condition of the period of detention;
- the nature of the obstacles preventing deportation/removal;
- the steps taken by the Home Office to overcome such obstacles;
- the condition the detainee is kept in;
- the risk of absconding;

7 §46 of *I (Afghanistan)* [2002] EWCA Civ 888)

- the risk of offending
- the effect of detention on the detainee and his family;

These factors are a non-exhaustive checklist and cannot be considered a '*trump card*' in justifying detention as the courts have been at pains to highlight time and again.[8] There must be a process where all these factors are considered cumulatively and when it starts to look unlikely that deportation/removal will take place that then the detainee must be released. If the detainee is not released then he is in a strong position in which to claim his detention as unlawful.

The Court of Appeal in ***Fardous v SSHD [2015] EWCA Civ 931***[9] highlighted the need for '*proper scrutiny*' involving a fact specific assessment with reference to '*Hardial Singh*' principles, in particular, with reference to the reasonableness of any length of detention.

Two further decisions which consider the third principle include the cases of ***Ademiluyi v SSHD [2017] EWHC 935 (Admin)*** and ***BS v Secretary of State for the Home Department*** *[2018] EWHC 454 (Admin)*. In ***Ademiluyi***, Michael Fordham QC, sitting as a Deputy High Court Judge, having considered the guidance of the Supreme Court in ***Lumba*** highlighted the questions that ought to be asked with reference to an assessment of the third principle as follows:

> '*Viewed objectively and on the facts as they presented themselves to the Secretary of State at the relevant time, was there or was there not a realistic prospect of deportation during a time which in all the circumstances of this case would be a reasonable time? Was it*

8 *R(AS) Somalia v SSHD* [2019] EWHC 1831 (Admin) citing *R (MH) v SSHD* [2010] EWCA Civ 1112) and *R(Shafiq-ur-Rehman) v SSHD* [2013] EWHC 1280 (Admin)

9 §37-41 – *Fardous v SSHD* [2015] EWCA Civ 931 https://www.bailii.org/ew/cases/EWCA/Civ/2015/931.html

> *sufficiently clear that no realistic prospect of that kind arose such that the Secretary of State should have released rather than detained?*[10]

This case concerned detention of an individual subject to deportation, who had completed his custodial sentence having been convicted for immigration- offences. His challenge to deportation included the fact that he had a significant family and private life under Article 8 of the ECHR, having resided here for over fifteen years, with a wife and five children born in the UK, which were factors before the Secretary of State at the outset of his detention . The Judge found that had these factors been considered then the objectively reasonable conclusion, would have been that removal would not be possible within a reasonable period[11]. Although it may not always be the case, given the question under the third principle is 'forward-looking'[12] when viewing all the factors of this case 'objectively'[13] it was clear that detention was unlawful from the outset and the risks of re-offending and absconding were not '*trump cards*'.

In the case of ***BS***, dealing with the third principle, the Court held detention "*was not justified under the AAR policies nor was it consistent with the third Hardial Singh principle*".[14] The applicant was held in detention on the 15th October 2016, after being detected in the UK en-route to Canada. He claimed asylum but his claim was refused and certified on the 23rd November 2016, a request was also made to the Indian High commission for an emergency travel document (ETD). He was then assessed and by virtue of a Rule 35 report it was found that he may have been a victim of torture, but there was no

10 §62 – ***Ademiluyi v SSHD [2017] EWHC 935 (Admin)***

11 §76 ibid

12 §86 ibid

13 §89 ibid

14 §66 – ***BS v Secretary of State for the Home Department [2018] EWHC 454 (Admin)***

assessment of likely harm and a review on the 24th November 2016, concluded that his continued detention was deemed suitable under Chapter 55 of the EIG. The Courts as a result in considering this period found detention at that stage was lawful as the detention had been reviewed appropriately. By the date of the next review, the court held it ought to have been clear from the High Commission correspondence that there would be a delay in processing travel documents at their end, together with the fact that ***BS*** had lodged judicial review against the certification of the decision made by the Home Office, that removal would not therefore be effective within a '*reasonable period*' and there was failure to act with '*reasonable diligence*'.

Both these cases highlights the very fact specific exercise that the Courts seek to undertake weighing in a number of competing factors before finding detention is unlawful.

Hardial Singh Principles 4 – Reasonable Diligence and Expedition

This fourth principle considers the actions of the Home Office in relation to a failure to act with due diligence, in other words has there been an unjustifiable delay in the actions of the Home Office in relation to detention procedures such that it renders the detention unlawful. This would be by reference to the court's own assessment of the facts rather than the normal review of an executive decision that would be conducted on *Wednesbury* grounds[15]. Furthermore, simply by demonstrating that a certain process was unduly delayed would not be sufficient, an individual would have to demonstrate that the "*dividing line between mere administrative failing and unreas-*

15 See §48 of *R(Muqutaar) v Home Secretary* [2013] 1 WLR 649

onableness amounting to illegality" had been crossed and as a result of the failure they were held longer than they ought to have been[16].

In the case of ***Saleh*** [2013] **EWCA Civ 1378**_the challenge was with reference to the second principle of whether the detention was for a period which was reasonable in all circumstances and further the fourth principle whether there was a requirement for the Secretary of State to act with "*reasonable diligence and expedition*" to effect removal.[17] Whilst, the court found that the Secretary of State had failed to file evidence to provide any justification for administrative delay for over a 12-month period, applying the principles of ***Krasniqi v SSHD*** *[2011] EWCA Civ 1549* they took a restrictive approach finding there to be only an 8-month period as unlawful.[18]

The same restrictive approach was adopted in the more recent case of ***R (SB (Ghana)) v Secretary of State for the Home Department & Anor*** [2020] EWHC 668 (Admin) where the Court held that delay in dealing with the applicant's claim were simply '*administrative failing side of the line rather than on the illegality side of the line as described in Krasniqi*'[19]

ii Grace Periods

There is one further aspect that must be considered once a breach of one of the '*Hardial Singh* principles has been established. This is the 'grace period' given to the Secretary of State to facilitate the release of the detainee, during which time detention remains lawful. The Court of Appeal in ***R (on the application of AC (Algeria) v Secretary***

16 See §12 of *R (Krasniqi) v SSHD* [2011] EWCA Civ 1549

17 §21 and §33 of *Saleh* [2013] **EWCA Civ 1378**

18 §66 Ibid

19 §88 of ***R (SB (Ghana)) v Secretary of State for the Home Department & Anor*** [2020] EWHC 668 (Admin)

of State for the Home Department [2020] EWCA Civ 36 revisited guidance on the issue, of *'grace periods',* given to the Secretary of State, once detention had ceased to comply with the *'Hardial Singh'* principle. In particular, Irwin LJ giving judgment in the Court of Appeal was concerned with whether or not the other limits on the Secretary of State's powers, embodied in the second and fourth principles, had been breached[20] during this time.

Having reviewed the authorities available on periods of grace Irwin LJ concluded that:

> *... [1] that the "grace periods" are granted for practical purposes, reflecting the facts of each case and applying a test of reasonableness; [2] that this court has declined to set any overall or absolute limit to such a period as a "long-stop" for all purposes; [3] that the periods have more usually been short, often a few days, but running up to a month, and [4] that there has been some tendency for the periods to increase.*[21]

What this actually means is that once any of the relevant principles (second, third or fourth principle) are breached, then rightly the question that would arise is whether or not any further detention was lawful. The only basis on which the court concluded such detention would be lawful was for "a reasonable period" to put in place appropriate conditions for release. Each case would be fact specific, taking into account the risk to public as an important factor, but not the only factor to justify indefinite immigration detention.[22] More importantly the Court highlighted that if a question of a period of grace arose in any case, then it would be the Respondent to advance

20 §29 of *R (on the application of AC (Algeria) v Secrteary of State for the Home Department* [2020] EWCA Civ 36

21 §33 Ibid

22 §38 & §39, ibid.

their case as to relevant period, and the reasons why such a period was appropriate.[23]

This judgement certainly mirrors the approach taken by the First-tier Tribunal, hearing bail applications during the lockdown due to COVID-19. The Home Office sought to criticise the Tribunal for granting a 'surprising' number of bail applications, releasing a large number of detainees during the start of the emergency period, one of the complaints raised by the Home Office was:

> *'that the current situation may make it difficult for us to source suitable accommodation if stipulated as part of a grant of Bail in Principle. There are particular challenges at the moment in finding properties which meet the Probation Service requirements where a person is subject to licence conditions[24]'*

The First-tier Tribunal of the Immigration and Asylum Chamber President[25], was unimpressed and highlighted,

> *"sourcing suitable accommodation when a person is subject to licensed conditions, this is a matter for UKVI, the criminal authorities and the probation service. I do not consider a refusal of bail application to be in accordance with the law, due to an inability of government departments, or those answerable to meet criminal license conditions."[26]*

---

23 §44 ibid.

24 Correspondence between the Home Office and the President of the FtT(IAC) in relation to bail grants. Document dated 29th April 2020 – https://ilpa.org.uk/wp-content/uploads/2020/05/Letter-to-MC-29.04.20-1.pdf

25 Mr Michael Clements

26 Correspondence between the Home Office and the President of the FtT(IAC) in relation to bail grants. Document dated 1st May 2020- https://ilpa.org.uk/correspondence-between-the-home-office-and-the-president-of-the-fttiac/

He made clear that it was a matter for the Home Office to ensure their house was in order and failure to ensure suitable accommodation was not a good reason to refuse bail. Whilst the Tribunal does not make findings on whether detention was lawful, in the context of bail decisions, they do have a duty to consider whether continued detention would be necessary.

Therefore, where the Home Office reasons were based on suitability or availability of accommodation on release, this could impact on a decision of whether detention was lawful and whether the Home Office had exhausted the "reasonable period" to put such conditions in place thus rendering any detention beyond that period as unlawful.

OTHER LIMITATIONS TO DETENTION

This guide is concerned mainly with the '*Hardial Singh'* principle, which affords the greatest protection against those claiming to be unlawfully detained. It is often accompanied by a claim that there has been breach of public law principles based on breach of Home office policy and rules (refer to Chapter3 for more detail). However, it would be remiss not to mention other potential routes through which detention can be challenged. These include but are not limited to:

i A potential breach under the Human Rights Act 1998, the most common being under Article 5 of the ECHR, which has been covered above briefly. In addition, the courts have also considered a breach of Article 3 of the ECHR, where the detention of a mentally ill person amounted to inhuman and degrading treatment and false imprisonment[27], and was irrational. Article 8 of the ECHR is also often pleaded where detention involves a failure to consider the impact of detention on children of a detainee as was the case in ***R(Abdollahi) v SSHD [2013] EWCA Civ 366***[28]

ii A potential breach under the laws that govern the European Union (EU) although with exit from the EU, such breaches may only be relevant to historical detention cases, depending on transitional arrangements and any other deals that may be made between the EU and the UK. In the recent cases of ***Hemmati v Secretary of State for the Home Department*** *[2019] UKSC 56* the Supreme court found detention of asylum seekers pending their removal to an EU state by virtue of the Dublin III Regulations[29], was unlawful given they failed to provide protection to those being transferred under a new Dublin regulation. It was held that Chapter 55 in relation to the Home Office policies did not satisfy the requirements imposed by Dublin III, that permitted detention where there was "*significant risk of absconding as defined by Dublin III*". The UK had failed to implement any new specific protections within Chapter 55 to protect those being transferred between member states under a new Dublin III Regulation. The court held that in these circumstances "*the decision to detain…lay outside the boundaries of any permissible exercise of the power to detain conferred by paragraph*

27 §173 – 181 ***R (on the application of HA (Nigeria)) v Secretary of State for the Home Department*** **[2012] EWHC 979 (Admin)**

28 See § 36 – 45 and the failure to take into account the best interests of the children under section 55 of the Borders citizenship and Immigration Act 2009.

29 See Article 28 – Regulation (EU) No 604/2013 Of The European Parliament And Of The Council of 26 June 2013 - https://eur-lex.europa.eu/LexUriServ/LexUriServ.do?uri=OJ:L:2013:180:0031:0059:EN:PDF

16(2) of Schedule 2 to the 1971 Act"[30]. The impact of this decision will only affect a small proportion of individuals who were detained for the purposes of Dublin III removal between the coming into force of the Dublin III Regulation in January 2014 through to 15 March 2017, when further regulations had been introduced by the Secretary of State[31].

iii The Equality Act 2010, more particularly section 149, also plays an important part in detention cases with reference to individuals who may have '*protected characteristics*'. In the case of ***R (on the application of HA (Nigeria)) [2012] EWHC 979 (Admin)*** decided prior to the introduction of the Equality Act 2010, the court found there was a breach of policy, which was in place from 2010 (found in Chapter 55.10 of the Enforcement Immigration Guidance) for certain categories of person considered unsuitable for detention. The court held that this policy in relation to detention of people with mental illness was unlawful and in breach of the Defendant's duties under section 71 of the Race Relations Act 1976 and section 49A of the Disability Discrimination Act 2005. These provisions now repealed by the Equality Act 2010, but section 149 of the Act provides similar protections . In the case of ***R(ASK) v SSHD*** **[2019] EWCA Civ 1239** the Court found there was a breach of the public sector equality duty by failing to make any reasonable adjustments based on the detainee's mental capacity. This case, provides an excellent understanding on the application of these provisions and ought to be considered detail if such a

30 §89 of ***Hemmati v Secretary of State for the Home Department*** *[2019] UKSC 56*

31 Following the CJEU judgement in *Al Chodor* C-528/15 the Secretary of State issued the Transfer for Determination of an Application for International Protection (Detention) (Significant Risk of Absconding Criteria) Regulations 2017 to be considered when identifying a significant risk of absconding.

claim is to be pursued with reference to a claim for unlawful detention[32]

32 ***R(ASK) v SSHD*** [2019] **EWCA Civ 1239** see in particular §76-§79, §130-136, §240-§245

CHAPTER THREE
HOME OFFICE POLICIES AND RULES

As already highlighted there are three main policies relevant to detention, some dealing specifically with the more vulnerable categories:

i. Chapter 55 – Detention and temporary release (formerly) Enforcement Instructions and Guidance[1] – the main policy that ought to be followed by the Home Office.

ii. Chapter 55a – Detention of Pregnant Women dated 12th July 2016 – Enforcement Instructions and Guidance[2] – a short policy document dealing specifically with pregnant women.

iii. Adult at Risk Policy[3] (also known as AAR policy)– an important policy reflecting calls for greater protections for those vulnerable being held in detention.

It is important to examine these policies in some detail in order to understand the process of detention as well as, the restrictions and safeguards to detention provided for, under our domestic laws as this will help you navigate whether someone may have been unlawfully

1 https://assets.publishing.service.gov.uk/government/uploads/system/uploads/attachment_data/file/804785/Chapter-55-detention-v26.0ext.pdf – Chapter 55

2 https://assets.publishing.service.gov.uk/government/uploads/system/uploads/attachment_data/file/653012/Chapter_55a_Detention_of_pregnant_women_v1.pdf – Chapter 55A

3 This Adult at Risk Policy is derived from two documents; the Policy Statement of July 2018 and Home Office Guidance used by caseworkers, which will be considered in some detail below.

detained. At the end of this chapter, the courts approach in relation to public law errors will be explored in more detail.

i <u>Chapter 55 – Detention and temporary release (formerly) Enforcement Instructions and Guidance</u>

At the outset of Chapter 55, the general principles explain the purpose of the policy in relation to detention. It highlights that detention must be reserved for matters which are in the interests of maintaining effective immigration control, with a presumption in favour of immigration bail and/or any alternatives to detention. It mirrors the statutory considerations already highlighted above in relation to when detention would be most appropriate as follows:

- To effect removal;
- To establish identity or basis of a claim made;
- Concerns as to an individual's ability to comply with conditions attached to bail

It acknowledges '*special consideration*' cases involving families, where there are children under the age of 18, as well as unaccompanied children, whose detention may have to be authorised until handed over to an appropriate carer, or where they are being removed.[4]

4 Refer to footnote 35 – All decisions concerning children would require an assessment of section 55 of the Borders, Citizenship and Immigration Act 2009, to ensure they are safeguarding and promoting the welfare of any child present in the UK.

Foreign National Offenders

Considering cases which involve foreign national offenders who have been detained following deportation action, it is made clear that *'substantial weight'* should be given to an assessment of an individual's risk of further offending or harming the public, which is assessed by reference to the seriousness of an individual's criminality, normally the trigger for deportation action in the first place.[5] Therefore making clear that ultimately the public protection is crucial to the policy on detention.

In relation to limitation on detention, the guidance refers to that which is implied by domestic and ECHR case law derived from Article 5 and Article 8 of the ECHR. In looking at an interference with family life under Article 8 of the ECHR, detention would not be lawful if it exceeded the period reasonably necessary for the purpose of removal/or where the interference with family life could be shown to be disproportionate.[6]

There must be a balancing exercise where the Home Office considers all factors relevant to an individual case, weighing them against particular risks of reoffending and of absconding for making an assessment of what is *'reasonably necessary'*. The more serious an offence the greater the weight attached to this factor when assessing if detention is reasonably necessary keeping in mind that in a non-criminal case a reasonable period for detention will be much shorter then in a criminal case.

There policy sets out a number of other factors which influence a decision to detain[7] and these factors must be kept under review regularly to ensure continued detention is justified. These include:

5 Chapter 55 – §55.1.3

6 ibid § 55.3.A

7 ibid § 55.3.1

- Likelihood of removal
- Previous absconding or risk of offending (usually to be assessed through National Offender Management Service (NOMS) unless no Offender Assessment System report.
- Previous failure to comply with bail conditions or a breach of immigration laws
- Previous history of compliance with immigration controls
- Ties to the UK; family, friends, employment etc.
- Outstanding appeals etc which will act as incentive to comply with conditions of release
- Whether the detainee is under 18 or an adult at risk.

It is important to note that decisions relating to detention or a grant of bail must follow certain processes and procedures, which includes the necessity for ensuring certain kinds of decisions are made by authorised Home Office officials [8]. If they are not this is certainly a factor which ought to form part of the background to any claim that detention has not been lawfully authorised.

Relevant Detention Forms

As already highlighted, there must be a regular review of detention as the circumstances of someone being detained may change such that their detention cannot continue to be justified.

8 ibid §55.3.2.2 and §55.5

At the outset reasons for detention must be recorded in writing and the detainee provided with a copy of the same, thereafter further written reasons, at monthly intervals reasons for continued detention.

The most relevant forms include:

- IS 91RA – this is issued with the initial risk assessment carried out, in particular the level of risk to themselves and others in detention, with an ongoing assessment during detention, issuing a new IS 91RA if there are changes to these factors over time.

- IS91 – this document is issued as the 'detention authority' and will contain a photograph of the detainee together with identified risk factors

- IS91R – this is the document that will contain the reasons for detention[9] and it is usually the most important document relevant to ensuring detention is justified. The form itself comprises of three parts, this must be completed in full, ensuring it sets out the basis on which the decision was made and that these reasons are fully understood by the detainee (in a language they fully understand). The reasons given for detention and ensuring correct protocol when this document is served on a detainee, are subject to judicial scrutiny in the event there was a challenge to an individual's detention. There are five standard reasons given for detention, which are set out on the form and thirteen standard factors which are meant to justify the reason given for detention. This is often a good starting point when examining whether detention is correctly mandated.

9 ibid §55.6.3

Reviews

It is important that detention reviews are carried out throughout the detention process, to ensure that it remains lawful and in line with policy at all times. Rule 9 of the Detention Centre Rules 2001 (DCR 2001) requires monthly written reviews that should be set out in a IS151F. For detainees held in short-term holding facilities, the corresponding rule is Rule 12 of the Short-term Holding Facility Rule 2018 (STHFR 2018). The guidance itself at §55.8 sets out comprehensive details of arrangements (see Tables 1 to 3) in relation to reviews for categories of detainees.

There is a specific duty with reference to the health and vulnerabilities of detainees, which are contained in rule 35 of the DCR 2001, and rule 32 of the STHFR 2018 and these will be considered below in chapter 4.

Special Cases

The guidance is also quite clear that there are a number of special cases[10] which include:

- Pregnant women
- spouses/civil partners of British citizens/EEA national[11]
- Unaccompanied young persons and individuals claiming to be under 18 (if detained as an adult, but later proved that they were a minor, could potentially bring a claim)[12]

---

10 ibid § 55.9

11 ibid §55.9.2

12 ibid §55.9.3.1 for more detail on issues arising where individuals claim to be under the age of 18

- Families with children under the age of 18[13].

The general position for EAA nationals and their family members, who may be subject to any administrative action, is that they should not be detained[14]. However, those being considered for deportation may be detained under the EEA Regulations 23(6)(b).

The guidance also covers in detail the position of foreign national offenders, who have completed their prison sentence, including where they can be detained, as well as those who may be subject to administrative removal but may be facing criminal proceedings against them, however, detailed consideration is not necessary for the issues considered within this guide.[15]

If an individual was being held pending an appeal hearing, and subsequently succeeded with reference to that appeal, the Home Office could challenge that decision, and continue to detain the individual as long as the decision to continue detention was fully reasoned.[16] There would however, be a strong case for immigration bail to be considered pending any further appeal.

---

13 ibid - §55.9.4

14 ibid - § 55.9.5

15 ibid - § 55.10 - §55.11

16 ibid - § 55.12.2

ii Adults at Risk Policy

This policy was instituted pursuant to section 59 of the Immigration Act 2016[17] and its aim was to ensure that those who were vulnerable and considered '*at risk*', were properly identified and **if** detained then this was with the relevant safeguards in place. It was introduced by the Government in response to the report by Stephen Shaw[18], reviewing the welfare of vulnerable people in detention. The Policy compromises of the statement issued in July 2018, Immigration Act 2016: Guidance on adults at risk in immigration detention[19] and is reinforced by guidance; Adult at risk in immigration detention.[20]

It continues to be the cornerstone of most challenges to detention. The general principles set out above in Chapter 55, do still apply however, this policy covers, in detail the circumstances of those individuals who may be regarded as risk as follows:

---

17 **Immigration Act 2016 – section 59 Guidance on detention of vulnerable persons**

(1) The Secretary of State must issue guidance specifying matters to be taken into account by a person to whom the guidance is addressed in determining—

(a) whether a person ("P") would be particularly vulnerable to harm if P were to be detained or to remain in detention, and

(b) if P is identified as being particularly vulnerable to harm in those circumstances, whether P should be detained or remain in detention.

18 **Review into the Welfare in Detention of Vulnerable Persons; A report to the Home Office by Stephen Shaw – January 2016 - https://assets.publishing.service.gov.uk/government/uploads/system/uploads/attachment_data/file/490782/52532_Shaw_Review_Accessible.pdf**

19 https://assets.publishing.service.gov.uk/government/uploads/system/uploads/attachment_data/file/721237/Adults_at_risk_in_immigration_detention_-_statutory_guidance__2_.pdf

20 The current version at the time of writing this is the **Adults at risk in detention Version 5.0 dated 6th March 2019** https://assets.publishing.service.gov.uk/government/uploads/system/uploads/attachment_data/file/784634/adults-at-risk-policy-v5.0ext.pdf

- They are clearly vulnerable to harm as a result of their previous experiences, such as torture, sexual violence or trafficking, and/or they are suffering from a particular condition;

- There is medical or professional evidence to demonstrate they are vulnerable in light of previous trauma suffered and/or are suffering from a certain condition that would render them vulnerable to harm in detention, whether or not an individual has highlighted this themselves

- Staff at the detention centre have observed behaviour which leads them to believe an individual is at risk.

There are certain *'indicators of risk'* which should alert a decision maker to certain vulnerabilities of individuals being detained. The guidance deals with the issues as listed below, in some detail, which are useful to consider in determining if an individual was appropriately identified as vulnerable, with relevant adjustments being made by the decision maker before the decision to detain was made. These factors are as follows:

- Serious physical disability;

- Serious physical health conditions or illnesses;

- Mental health conditions;

- Torture victims;

- Potential victims of trafficking on modern slavery;

- Age (in particular anyone over the age of 70 is to be considered at risk);

- Pregnant women;

- Transsexual and intersex people.

The guidance is comprehensive in considering the remit of factors relevant to each category and assessing whether the facts of an individual case would justify detention. However, at the same time the guidance makes clear that list of indicators of those at risk is not limited to those identified in the guidance, but may will include other individuals. So long as there is an assessment on the likely risk of harm to an individual based on the evidence available then detention may be sustainable.

The guidance appears to ascribe a hierarchical system to the different forms of evidence that may be produced to demonstrate an individual is vulnerable and at risk. The stronger the evidence the greater the weight that can be ascribed to it in determining the risk of harm, whilst in detention. The three levels of evidence are as follows:

i. Level 1 – at the lowest level and of limited weight in being able to secure detention is a self-declaration by an individual or his representative of a certain vulnerability and for example can take place during screening process for an asylum claim

ii. Level 2 – this level includes professional evidence for example from; medical practitioners, non-government organisations and social workers, which should be accepted as demonstrating the impact of detention on an individual. This is to be accorded some weight but will be weighed up against other factors such as; whether removal is imminent, an individual's history of non/compliance, other public protection concern

iii. Level 3 – At the highest level of evidence is that which is produced from professionals (as above) which specifies specifically that an individual would be a risk and identifying that a period of detention would likely cause harm.

If there is no *'realistic prospect of removal within a reasonable timescale'*, then detention is not justified. However, where a timescale has been identified for removal, then each case will considered on its own specific facts, assessing the level of evidence produced to determine vulnerability to be balanced against the immigration factors, including i) length of time in detention to effect removal; ii) previous compliance with immigration controls and iii) any public protection issues that arise.

Where, Level 1 evidence is produced then detention would be justified, if either:

- date of removal can be forecast with some certainty,
- someone's presence in the UK is identified as not conducive to the public good
- there is some indication of non-compliance

In relation to Level 2 evidence, the factors required to justify detention are narrower in their scope, as follows:

- a date for removal must be fixed/fixable at short notice
- the concerns around public protection are high, for reasons of criminality, national security etc

- there are specific negative indicators of non-compliance demonstrating such that it is *'highly likely'* individual would not be removed unless detained

Evidence, which is identified at Level 3, makes it difficult to justify continued detention. Where such evidence is available, it ought to be accorded its due weight with reference to an individual's vulnerability and in particular where medical evidence exists, then it is of *'significant potential value'*[21] such that it should not be doubted as a source of corroborating an individual's vulnerability unless the evidence was previously rejected by an independent tribunal or credibility issues arise from other sources.

Continued detention in all the circumstances would only be justified if (i) a date for removal had been set with no barriers to removal and all arrangements in place to ensure safe return (ii) there were significant public protection concerns or if an individual had been subject to a minimum 4 year sentence or there were national security concerns.

One of the most important factors in determining if vulnerable individuals should indeed be detained, is the length of likely detention. Further alternative measures to detention should also form part of the assessment of whether an individual should be detained. These include residence or reporting restrictions when removal is being planned/arranged to ensure detention of any individual who might be at risk, is kept to a minimum.

As per any other detained case, there must be an ongoing assessment of risk to ensure that any new factors are taken into account, which may make the detention inappropriate.

---

21 See *KV (Sri Lanka) [2019] UKSC 10*

The mechanism of a Rule 35 of the Detention Centre Rules 2001 report and Rule 32 of the Short-term Holding Facility Rule report, is very important for particularly vulnerable detainees, and identifying those who might be at risk are brought to the attention of the authorities as soon as possible (refer to chapter 4).

Such a report is considered, level 3 evidence and as already highlighted if it is not followed, where an individual is identified as vulnerable and an individual is not released, then this is a very good ground for securing bail and in the alternative challenging detention by way of judicial review proceedings.

This guidance also highlights a very important source of information, when contemplating any form of action in relation to detention, that is the Home Office, Case Information Database (CID), which requires a record of all assessments made in detention to be recorded.

Covid-19, saw the immigration authorities introduce special statutory guidance[22] in order to comply with guidance issued by Public Health England (PHE) on 16 March 2020[23]. In particular, it ensured a further assessment of any individual who was considered an adult at risk, in line with the latest PHE guidance and any factor which may have caused an increased risk of illness as a result of coronavirus. Therefore any detention or continued detention during this period would be subject to additional scrutiny to safeguard those who were considered to be at risk. The guidance would have been

22 Detention considerations: COVID-19 -https://www.gov.uk/government/publications/adults-at-risk-in-immigration-detention/detention-considerations-covid-19

23 'COVID-19: Prisons and other places of detention' – https://www.gov.uk/government/publications/covid-19-prisons-and-other-prescribed-places-of-detention-guidance/covid-19-prisons-and-other-prescribed-places-of-detention-guidance

subject to change as the guidance on restrictions generally during this period was constantly evolving. It would therefore be good practice to identify the guidance, which was applicable at the time of detention, where damages are sought for any historical period of detention. The same is true of any of the Home Office policies and one can often find old policies in the Home Office archives[24].

Failure to comply with this guidance is a common challenge seen by the Courts, with common issues being raised relating to failure to properly categorise evidence produced, such that an individual is not recognised as someone at risk, or alternatively having recognised someone to be at risk, but detention was still seen as justified.

The follow-up report by Stephen Shaw in July 2018[25] highlighted the failings of the Adult at Risk policy, which is reflected by the high levels of challenges seen in relation to the application of the policy for the purposes of justifying deportation.

iii Chapter 55A – Detention of pregnant women – 12th July 2016

As the policy title suggests, this guidance covers pregnant women, which is clearly indicative of the fact that pregnant women may be detained and removed. There is a preference of course for women who are pregnant, without any basis to remain in the UK to leave voluntarily. Section 60 of the Immigration Act 2016, sets out the

24 https://webarchive.nationalarchives.gov.uk/*/http:/www.ukba.homeoffice.gov.uk/

25 Assessment of government progress in implementing the report on the welfare in detention of vulnerable persons – A follow-up report to the Home Office by Stephen Shaw – July 2018
https://assets.publishing.service.gov.uk/government/uploads/system/uploads/attachment_data/file/728376/Shaw_report_2018_Final_web_accessible.pdf

safeguards and limitations of detaining pregnant women and the guidance at Chapter 55a provides assistance on its scope.

In particular, if the Secretary of State is satisfied a woman is pregnant, then they cannot detain her unless i) she would shortly be removed from the United Kingdom[26] or there were exceptional circumstances, which justified the detention.[27]

In particular, there is a time limit for the detention of a pregnant woman of up to 72 hours. Beyond this period, detention is only permitted limited for up to 7 days if authorised by Minister of the Crown.[28]

The very exceptional circumstances to justify detention of a pregnant woman, who would not be removed imminently is restricted to those who are a risk to the public or had breached conditions of bail and/or detained under Section 36 (1) of the UK Borders Act 2007, pending a decision on whether automatic deportation provisions applied to them. In addition there is also a duty to consider the welfare concerns of a pregnant woman.

The Secretary of State would have to be satisfied of the pregnancy either by way of credible medical documentary evidence confirming the same unless they were visibly pregnant. It would be essential to know the date at which the Secretary of State become aware, as it is relevant to calculating the permitted length of detention. There is also nothing to stop a pregnant woman who has been released from being re-detained as long as the Section 60, is complied with.

---

26 s.60(2)(a) of the Immigration Act 2016

27 s.60(2)(b) of the Immigration Act 2016

28 s.60(4)(a) of the Immigration Act 2016

Policy Challenges

Detention will always be considered lawful so long as it is premised on one of the statutory powers and within the confines of domestic and Strasbourg caselaw whilst at the same time complying with relevant policy.

Summarising above the various policies that deal with detention it is clear, the Home Office powers to detain are technically limited, with detention being used as a 'last resort' and the presumption always in favour of release. The policies highlighted above set out general principles in relation to detention and further highlight the safeguards for a number of categories of individuals. Where detention is maintained in breach of any of these policies then this is certainly a weighty factor in demonstrating detention is unlawful.

The Supreme Court gave authoritative guidance in the case of ***R (Lumba & Mighty) v Secretary of State for the Home Department*** *[2011] UKSC 12* and ***SK (Zimbabwe) v Secretary of State for the Home Department*** *[2011] UKSC 23* (***Kambadzi***) in relation to the limits of detention. Parts of the decision relevant to the 'Hardial Singh' principles have already been set out above. The case of ***Lumba & Mighty*** involved consideration of detention in breach of an unpublished policy under which, the Home Office sought in to detain foreign national offenders and in ***Kambadzi***, there had been a failure to carry out reviews as was required by rule 9(1) of the Detention Centre Rules 2001 and policy contained in the Operations Enforcement Manual. Both cases concerned detention pending deportation. It was acknowledged that the breach of a material policy, or making a decision by reference to an unlawful policy would amount to a public law error.[29] The test to demonstrate such a

29 §26 of ***Lumba*** and §39-42 of ***Kambadzi*** by reference to ***R (Nadarajah) v Secretary of State for the Home Department [2003] EWCA Civ 1768, [2004]***

breach, was to consider if the error was material to the decision taken to detain, that is whether the breach of public law bore on and was relevant to the decision to detain such that it vitiated the authority to detain[30]. Furthermore, where detention was found to be lawful, the question of whether the detention would have occurred in any case, would have been relevant to the question of damages. In ***Lumba*** the court held he would only to be entitled to nominal damages as he would have been lawfully detained pending deportation in any case. The amount in damages may well be a consideration for individuals starting a claim for false imprisonment especially when considered against the stress of litigation, particularly for those who may be vulnerable in the first place.. Although, in some cases individuals may simply be seeking a declaration of unlawful detention.

The more recent decision of the Supreme Court in ***DN (Rwanda) v Secretary of State for the Home Department [2020] UKSC 7*** endorsed the public law principles, set out in ***Lumba*** and ***Kambadzi.*** The Court further considered in line with ***Lumba***[31] that there was no difference:

> *between (i) a detention which is unlawful because there was no statutory power to detain and (ii) a detention which is unlawful because the decision to detain, although authorised by statute, was made in breach of a rule of public law.*

Therefore, where detention pending deportation was unlawful and the decision to make a deportation order and the deportation order were both based on a statutory instrument that was later declared to be ultra vires[32] then they were made in breach of a rule of public law. This overturned the decision made in ***R (Draga) v Secretary of State***

INLR 139

30 §68 of ***Lumba*** and §39-40 of ***Kambadzi***

31 §66

32 *EN (Serbia) v SSHD* [2009] EWCA Civ 630

for the Home Department [2012] EWCA Civ 842 where it was held that detention was separate to a decision to deport.

This was an important decision not only endorsing the ***Lumba*** principles, but also to ensuring that there remains an accountability for decisions in breach of public law principles.

CHAPTER FOUR
MEDICAL ASSESSMENTS IN DETENTION

Rule 35 and Rule 32 Reports

It is worth mentioning here, the Detention Centre Rules (DCR) 2001, as amended by the Detention Centre (amendment) Rules 2018[1] are almost identical to the Short-term Holding Facility Rules 2018,[2] both are relevant with reference to ensuring that those who may be vulnerable are brought to the attention of the detaining authorities as soon as possible and their detention is reviewed accordingly. For the purpose of this chapter, the main focus will be on Rule 35, which is more commonly seen in challenges to detention. Helpful guidance on the preparation and consideration of reports can be found within the Home office guidance on Detention services order 09/2016 Detention centre rule 35 and Short- term Holding Facility rule 32[3].

Under Rule 34 of the DCR 2001, it is mandatory for each detainee to be given physical and mental examination within 24 hours of their admission to the detention centre by a GP. A failure on behalf of the detaining authorities to ensure such an examination takes place, can render detention unlawful[4] although the courts have made clear that each case is fact specific and the '*question that has to be considered is*

---

1 https://www.legislation.gov.uk/uksi/2001/238/article/35/made

2 https://www.legislation.gov.uk/uksi/2018/409/contents/made

3 Published on the 5th March 2019 – https://assets.publishing.service.gov.uk/government/uploads/system/uploads/attachment_data/file/783642/Detention_rule_35_process.pdf

4 Rule 34(1) – see also the case of *R (SW) v Secretary of State for the Home Department* [2018] EWHC (Admin) §87-89

whether, had the Rule 34 medical examinations been carried out when they should have been would they have led to the claimant's earlier release?[5]

Such an examination can only take place with the consent of a detainee and in accordance with Rule 35, the medical practitioner, by way of a report must set out any concerns in relation to the following matters:

i. Anyone whose health '*is likely to be injuriously affected by continuous detention*',[6] which if reported by way of Rule 35, is to be considered, Level 3 evidence

ii. Anyone who is suspected of having suicidal intentions,[7] with a requirement for such an individual to be placed under special observation for the record of any treatment, for as long as those suspicions remained. However, such evidence will not always necessitate a review of appropriateness of detention

iii. Anyone who may have been a victim of torture,[8] a declaration of which will amount to Level 2 evidence at the very least. Such a report need not comply with the Istanbul Protocol, but will be placed on a detainee's medical record.

Once the report is completed it would have to be sent to the Secretary of State, without any delay[9] and it would also be compulsory for any medical practitioner to '*pay special attention to a detained*

5 *KG, R (On the Application Of) v Secretary of State for the Home Department [2018] EWHC 1767 (Admin) (13 July 2018)* §27-29

6 Rule 35(1)

7 Rule 35(2)

8 Rule 35(3)

9 Rule 35(4)

individual whose mental health required it making any special arrangements, which would include counselling which appeared necessary for provision or care of such an individual'[10].

Reports under Rule 35 can only be prepared and submitted by doctors, however other health professionals including, nurses could report any claims made by detainees, such that they had been a victim of torture, which would then lead to an appointment with a doctor.

Definition of Torture

Any assessment to be made in relation a claim of torture must be in accordance with Rule 35(6), which provides the definition as:

> *'any act by which a perpetrator intentionally inflicts severe pain or suffering on a victim in a situation in which-*
>
> *(a) the perpetrator has control (whether mental or physical) over the victim and*
>
> *(b) as a result of that control the victim is powerless to resist*[11].'

It is important to note here that previously, only those who were victims of torture at the hands of the state could fall within the terms of the guidance, until a challenge to the High Court in the case of ***Medical Justice [2017] EWHC 2461 (Admin)***, where Ousley J, declared limiting the definition of the term torture in the Adult at Risk Policy unlawful, where it excluded torture perpetrated by those

10 Rule 35(5)

11 There is no difference between the term 'powerless to resist' found under rule 35(6)(b) of the DCR 2001 and the term 'powerlessness' found under rule 32(6)(b) of the STHFR 2018

considered non-state actors. He held that the definition was unlawful because it '*lacked a rational or evidence base*' and it '*would require medical practitioners to reach conclusions on political issues which they cannot rationally be asked to reach*'"[12] The resultant challenge led to parts of the adults at risk guidance being declared unlawful and therefore withdrawn and re-issued in its current amended form.

The process that follows completion of a rule 35 report, starts with the medical practitioner forwarding it to the Detention Engagement Team (DET) who will then, forward a copy of the detainee's legal representative as well as the Home office responsible officer (within 24 hours of receipt) and these matters ought to be recorded on the CID, as well as the immigration removal centre's rule 35 log. Once the responsible officer in the Home Office receives this report, then in line with the Adults at Risk policy they would have two working days after accepting receipt in order review detention and to respond to the detainee's legal representative, with reasons if detention is being maintained.

Often detainees and their representatives may send in medical legal reports, which allege that a detainee has been a victim of torture. These must again be considered in light of the Adults at Risk guidance, and a doctor ought to review whether or not such a report is sufficient for them to make Rule 35 report.

When requesting an independent medico-legal report on behalf a detainee, it is important for any instructions to medical professionals to focus on the definitions of those who are considered vulnerable as set out within the policy. Where such evidence is produced the guidance highlights that '*very strong reasons*' would be needed to disagree with such evidence.

---

12 §192 of *Medical Justice [2017] EWHC 2461 (Admin)*

This position is reinforced by the discovery of unpublished guidance on detaining vulnerable migrants. This came to light following a Freedom of Information request[13] in a case where the court was being asked to determine the lawfulness of the approach to the medico-legal report, which disclosed the detainee was suffering with PTSD and depression, and continued detention was detrimental to his health, therefore such evidence ought to have been be accorded Level 3 evidence under the Adult at Risk policy. The Home Office provided evidence from a medical profession to the contrary. The case was eventually settled by consent given the terms of the unpublished policy were in clear contradiction with the Home Office's position. The documents disclosed included 1) Adults at Risk Returns Assurance Team - '*Medico-Legal Reports (MLR) – Guidance and Frequently Asked Questions* dated June 2018; 2) An email chain dated June 2018; 3) An email chain dated December 2018[14].

This guidance now helpfully confirms that any medico-legal report being assessed under the Adult at Risk policy by case workers should not be challenged unless there were '*clear mistakes or errors*' and that they should '*not specifically challenge the doctor's clinical opinion*' thereby recognizing they were an expert in their field. Further that a recent medico-legal report in conflict with an older assessment in a Rule 35 report, ought to be preferred.

The discovery and general dissemination of this policy and instructions to Home Office caseworkers is a timely reminder of Supreme Courts guidance on the value of medical reports and how such evidence can be of "significant potential value"[15] especially in light of

---

13 Freedom of information requests made by Lewis Kett of Duncan Lewis Solicitors

14 See Freedom of information report and response at https://www.duncanlewis.co.uk/onlinelinks/MLR%20Guidance%20in%20AAR%20Cases%20-%20FOI%20Response%20and%20Disclosure.pdf

15 *KV (Sri Lanka) v Secretary of State for the Home Department* [2019] UKSC 10

the numerous complaints that the rule 35 system did not work with a vast majority of reports not leading to any change in detention.[16]

The importance of judicial oversight in light of these concerns is evident and in fact the courts did consider the rule 35 system in the case ***IS (Bangladesh) [2019] EWHC 2017 (Admin)*** however, found that despite its failings, rule 35 of the Detention Centre Rules 2001, was not *ultra vires* or irrational.

16 Report by the Home Affairs Committee and Immigration Detention dated 21st March 2019 highlighted the concerns in relation to the rule 35 process, then called for an urgent overhaul of the governments Adults a Risk policy. The system itself was considered not to be independent or fair

CHAPTER FIVE
BAIL

General principles – Immigration Act 2016

Bail is a mechanism through which individuals can be released from detention. The Bail system was revised on the 15th January 2018, with changes effected by the Immigration Act 2016 (2016 Act) in particular, Sections 61(1) and 61(2) as well as, section 66 of the 2016 Act, with the main bail provisions set out in Schedule 10 of the 2016 Act. Schedule 10 sought to amalgamate a number of alternatives to detention, such as temporary admission, temporary release on bail and release on restrictions with one single power under which bail could be granted.

This framework under which immigration bail is now considered include the following statutory provisions and guidance:

- Schedule 10 to the Immigration Act 2016[1]
- Presidential guidance note No.1 of 2018 (guidance for FTT Judges)[2]
- First-tier Tribunal (Immigration and Asylum Chamber) Rules 2014[3]

---

1 https://www.legislation.gov.uk/ukpga/2016/19/contents/enacted

2 https://www.judiciary.uk/wp-content/uploads/2018/05/bail-guidance-2018-final.pdf

3 updated on the 1st February 2020 – https://assets.publishing.service.gov.uk/government/uploads/system/uploads/attachment_data/file/866217/consolidated-ftt-iac-rules-20200201.pdf

- Home Office guidance – Immigration bail v 5.0 (28th February 2020)[4]

Any person detained under statutory provisions set out in earlier chapters, are eligible to be granted bail by the Secretary of State or the First-tier Tribunal. Both the Secretary of State and the First-tier Tribunal derive their powers from schedule 10 to grant bail, the Secretary of State's powers are derived from paragraph 1(2), whereas the First-tier Tribunal from paragraph 1(3).

The Secretary of State's remit is wider than that of the Tribunal, in particular given the Secretary of State are able to grant bail to individuals who are liable to detention, that is they have not as yet been detained.

Schedule 10 (3)(2) specifically sets out matters that ought to be considered when determining whether to grant bail or subject an individual to certain conditions. These include:

- Risk of absconding
- Previous convictions
- Risk of reoffending
- Risk of harm to public if released
- "Such are the matters" that are considered relevant

These powers also restrict an application for bail being made in the first eight days, after arriving in the UK if they are detained subject

4 https://assets.publishing.service.gov.uk/government/uploads/system/uploads/attachment_data/file/869352/Immigration-bail-v5.0ext.pdf

to 16(1) of Schedule 2 to the Immigration Act 1971.[5] Further, where removal directions are in force for removal within fourteen days then consent of the Secretary of State is required before bail is granted.[6]

One of the peculiarities in relation to powers given to the Secretary of State under this schedule, is that they are permitted to grant bail where an individual can no longer be detained if they are liable to detention (that is there is no realistic prospect of their removal taking place within a reasonable time), under paragraph 10(1)(1) or where the Secretary of State is considering making a deportation under Section 5 (1) of the Immigration Act 1971[7]. This is contrary to the Supreme Court's decision, under the old statutory regime for granting bail, as was considered in the case of ***B (Algeria) v SSHD*** *[2018] UKSC 5*, where it was held that bail could not be granted to those who could not specifically be detained. Therefore, whilst, this ruling is no longer applicable it may still be of some limited application to historical claims of unlawful detention, where individuals may have found themselves in detention with no removal in sight.

A grant of bail in itself can be subject to specific conditions being arranged as provided for by Schedule 10 (3)(8). Conditions that may be imposed can include and are not limited to reporting restrictions, restrictions on work/studies, condition on residence[8], electronic monitoring[9], financial conditions[10] and any other conditions including curfew.

Schedule 10 (9)(2) deals specifically with accommodation and travel expenses which can be provided by the Secretary of State, but the test

5 Schedule 10 (3)(3),
6 Schedule 10 (3)(4)
7 Schedule 10 (1)(5),
8 Schedule 10 (9)
9 Schedule 10 (4)
10 Schedule 10 (5)

in relation to both is that there must be exceptional circumstances to justify provision of either.

In relation to powers that immigration officers have with reference to those believed to be in breach of immigration bail, Schedule 10(10), provides for an immigration officer or a constable to arrest a person on immigration bail if the immigration officer or constable has reasonable grounds for:

- believing that the person is likely to fail to comply with a bail condition
- suspecting that the person is failing, or has failed, to comply with a bail

If bail is granted by the Tribunal they could include a direction[11] to transfer management of bail to the Secretary of State. This allows Secretary of State to vary bail conditions, in which case there is no judicial scrutiny or oversight, if the Secretary of State seek to vary bail conditions to be more onerous then were set for by the Tribunal.

Where an individual is detained subject to paragraph 16 of Schedule 2 of the Immigration Act 1971 or Section 62 of the Nationality, Immigration and Asylum Act 2002, then Schedule 10(11) imposes a duty on the Secretary of State to make an automatic referral to the First-tier Tribunal for a decision on whether to grant immigration bail, within four months of first being detained (or in the alternative four months after the last bail consideration if no other bail applications have been made) and thereafter every four months.

The Tribunal is also directed under Schedule 10, to refuse all repeat bail applications repeat made 28 days from the last refusal of bail

11 Schedule 10 (6)

unless there has been a material change in an individual's circumstances.[12]

Presidential guidance note No 1 of 2018 (FTT bail guidance)

This guidance was introduced in order to provide assistance to Judges of the First-tier Tribunal, when hearing bail applications, given changes to immigration bail brought about by Schedule 10 Immigration Act 2016.

At the outset in its general principles at §4, the guidance highlights "*Liberty is a fundamental right of all people and can only be restricted if there is no reasonable alternative*". Whilst it makes clear that the First-tier Tribunal does not engage in considering whether detention is lawful, it helps frame the conditions in which detention can no longer be justified. Whilst, the guidance is not determinative, it helpfully sets out that it would be generally accepted that detention for three months would be considered quite a substantial period, whereas six months would be considered a long period which require imperative considerations of public safety in order to justify any continuing detention. [13]

It provides helpful and practical guidance as to the application of various parts of Schedule 10 of the Immigration Act 2016 from the matters to be considered as part of the bail application through to any conditions that may be imposed on an individual[14].

The Tribunal at the outset will make an assessment of an individual's likelihood of failing to comply with bail with the risk likely to be lowered where a removal is not imminent. In particular, this is often

12 Schedule 10 (12)
13 §7 of FTT bail guidance
14 §9-§15 of FTT bail guidance

assessed by virtue of any pending applications, but where removal is scheduled within fourteen days of the bail hearing, this may strengthen the fact that removal is imminent. Guidance on other relevant factors already listed above are also set out in the FTT Bail guidance in some detail and include an assessment of previous convictions, the risk of re-offending, possible danger to public health or a threat to maintenance of public order, and lastly whether the detention is necessary in that person's interest (avoiding the use of this power in place of remand or under the Mental Health Acts) or protection of others. All risks can certainly be met by suitable conditions such as residence conditions, reporting conditions, electronic monitoring, curfew and financial conditions.

Curfew

In the case of ***Gedi, R (On the Application Of) v Secretary of State for Home Department [2016] EWCA Civ 409 (17 May 2016)*** the Court of Appeal considered Secretary of State's power to impose conditions of curfew and electronic monitoring on those who had been released from immigration detention pending conclusion of deportation proceedings. Considering, schedules 2 & 3 of the Immigration Act 1971, it was held that there was no authority to impose a curfew as part of conditions of bail necessary. Following this, in the case of ***R (on the application of Jollah) v Secretary of State for the Home Department [2018] EWCA Civ 1260***[15] the Court of Appeal upheld an award of damages for false imprisonment, made in the High Court, where it was held that a curfew imposed by the Secretary of State having been released on immig-

15 Also upheld by the Supreme Court after the Secretary of State appealed. See **R (on the application of Jalloh (formerly Jollah) v SSHD [2020] UKSC 4**, where it was found that it is possible for there to be imprisonment at common law without a deprivation of liberty under article 5 of the ECHR

ration bail, requiring an individual to be present at a certain address between certain hours, was unlawful and gave rise to the tort of false imprisonment.

Accommodation

As already highlighted above, where bail is granted subject to accommodation being arranged by the Home Office, delay to the processing of an application for accommodation can be subject to scrutiny as that is the only condition pending subject to which bail would have been granted. This was certainly the case in ***R (Diop) v Secretary of State for the Home Department [2018] EWHC 1934 (Admin)***[16] where there had been a delay from the time he was granted bail in principle on 10th November 2017, subject to accommodation being arranged, to the 7th December 2017, when he was released. This period was found to be unlawful in particular when removal was no longer imminent in light of the Senegalese embassy's refusal to grant emergency travel documentation on the 9th November 2017.

The new bail regime certainly offers the Secretary of State greater powers in relation to the bail process, whilst, they have always had the power to refuse or grant bail in the first instance, as well as oppose bail at a bail hearing before the First-tier Tribunal, the mechanism of transferring bail management after a grant of bail appears to be an unnecessary oversight.

As already highlighted the Secretary of State can provide accommodation under Schedule 10(9), in "exceptional circumstances".

---

16 https://www.bailii.org/ew/cases/EWHC/Admin/2018/1934.html_ also refer to judgement on quantum ***Diop, R (On the Application Of) v Secretary of State for the Home Department*** [2018] EWHC 3420

However, in a recent case of ***Humnyntskyi v SSHD [2020] EWHC 1912 Admin***[17] it was held:

> *"...the Secretary of State's policy for granting Schedule 10 accommodation is unlawful because:*
>
> *(1) It is systemically unfair. It creates a real risk that unfair decisions will be made in a significant number of cases. Those risks materialised in the cases before the Court.*
>
> *(2) In its operation it fetters the Secretary of State's discretion to consider whether the situation of an individual applicant amounts to exceptional circumstances. That unlawful fetter was applied in the cases before the Court."*

One of the Claimant's in this case succeeded in establishing that the Secretary of State breached his rights under Article 3 of the ECHR[18], with the other two Claimant's establishing they had been unlawfully detained given the failure of the Secretary of State's refusal to arrange accommodation. This judgement will have a widespread impact on those foreign national offenders or other vulnerable individuals, who may have been denied or were awaiting a grant of accommodation as well as, those made homeless (and subject to rough sleeping) as a result of being denied accommodation.

In addition, the Secretary of State's failure to provide accommodation to asylum seekers under Section 95 or Section 98 of the Immigration Asylum Act 1999, as well as failed asylum seekers under

---

17 ***Humnyntskyi v SSHD***[2020] EWHC 1912 Admin §302

18 ibid §299 – Having refused Schedule 10 accommodation the Claimant became homeless and as a result had been able to demonstrate a real and immediate risk of suffering such that it was found the Secretary of State had breached his Article 3 rights under the ECHR and was entitled to a declaration to that effect and an award of damages by way of just satisfaction

Section 4 (2) of the Immigration Asylum Act 1999[19], families with dependent children who are provided accommodation to safeguard and promote welfare of children under Section 17 of the Children Act 1989 (or other equivalent provisions) and lastly, migrants accommodated under the Care Act 2014, may also lead to a breach of an individual's Article 3 rights

In the very recent case of ***Merca v SSHD [2020] EWCH 1479 (Admin)***[20], which was an application for interim relief, the High Court noted that Mr. Merca had been granted Section 95 accommodation where, the Secretary of State reversed their initial decision to have refused such accommodation on the 29th May 2020 (this was same date the Claimant instituted judicial review proceedings) but then acted very slowly in order to progress matters. The matter came before Fordham J on the 8th June 2020, who explored the delay from the 29th May 2020 to the 8th June 2020 in line with the with the Court of Appeals decision on grace periods in *AC (Algeria)*[21] which held that two weeks was sufficient for any arrangements of release to be concluded. The Secretary of State of State were therefore given the remainder of the week (which would bring them up to two weeks) in which to arrange accommodation.

The Court's decision to hold the Secretary of State accountable, by applying the latest guidance on grace periods strictly, is promising as it certainly demonstrates the Court's approach is to encourage the Secretary of State's actions to minimise any form of delay.

---

19 It is useful to consider the Home Office Guidance **Asylum support, section 4(2): policy and process 16th February 2018** https://assets.publishing.service.gov.uk/government/uploads/system/uploads/attachment_data/file/682495/asylum-support-section-4_2_-policy-and-process-v1.0ext.pdf

20 https://www.bailii.org/ew/cases/EWHC/Admin/2020/1479.html

21 [2020]EWCA Civ 36

The COVID-19 pandemic has impacted on all aspects of daily life, but more significantly the impact for those being detained, in particular the more vulnerable detainees that may be covered by various polices which have already been discussed. At the start of the restrictions, as a result of the pandemic, in the case of ***R (Detention Action & Anor) v SSHD [2020] EWHC 732 (Admin)*** a challenge was brought to "*the ongoing detention of all immigration detainees, in particular those with pre-existing conditions which increase vulnerability to COVID–19… [and]… the absence of an effective system for protecting immigration detainees from COVID–19*"[22]. Each judicial review was lodged on the 18th March 2020 and a decision on interim relief was given on the 25th March 2020. These were undoubtedly exceptional circumstances and the court examined carefully the provisions introduced by the Secretary of State in response to COVID-19 and compliance with the various new guidance managing the impact of COVID-19 in detention.

The High Court concluded that the "*The Secretary of State has put in place a process for detention reviews and is working to that system. As part of that system the Secretary of State has prioritised consideration of the position of those who fall into the increased-risk groups*"[23]. These actions by the Secretary of State were considered lawful, as they were acting within the powers set out under the new guidance. The Court further held that the evidence produced by the Claimants "*did not demonstrate an arguable case that maintaining the immigration detention system including the measures taken to date by the Secretary of State gives rise to a real risk of death or article 3 ill-treatment of persons who remain in detention*".[24]

---

22 ***R (Detention Action & Anor) v SSHD [2020] EWHC 732 (Admin)*** at §1

23 §19 ibid

24 §27 ibid

What the courts essentially found was that the risk from COVID in detention, was no different from the risk for the entire population and given the evolving situation they cautioned that, "*the golden rules are that representatives who bring claims must prepare those claims cogently and conduct the litigation sensibly and proportionately, and most of all, they must cooperate with each other when preparing cases and bringing them to the Court.*"[25] However, it was still important to have explored the position of those in detention who were made vulnerable by their very detention and potential conditions, with such an unpredictable virus.

Whilst, there was a wholesale rejection of the approach taken in this case, applications for bail during the pandemic had a more positive outcome, certainly Bail for Immigration Detainees (BiD) reported that they had a 91% success rate since the onset of the pandemic in relation to bail applications made and certainly more fact specific cases challenges for those being detained have met with success[26]

25 §32 ibid

26 See ***Samson Bello, R (On the Application Of) v The Secretary of State for the Home Department [2020] EWHC 950***

CHAPTER SIX
JUDICIAL REVIEW – UNLAWFUL DETENTION

Starting a Claim for Judicial Review

Judicial review is a challenge brought against the lawfulness of a decision or action made by a public body, which in the case of immigration cases is Home Office and the Secretary of State as her agent. The challenge is premised on the grounds that the decision of the Home Office was unlawful/illegal, irrational/unreasonable or simply unfair, breaching the principles of natural justice and it would be a matter for the court to review the decision in line with these guiding principles. Most judicial review challenges to immigration decisions are now brought in the Upper Tribunal (UT) in accordance with the Lord Chief Justice's, Consolidated Direction given in accordance with Part 1 of Schedule 2 to the Constitutional Reform Act 2005 and s. 18 of the Tribunals, Courts and Enforcement Act 2007[1]. However, claims to challenge the lawfulness of detention falls outside of the UT's judicial review jurisdiction, therefore any such challenge will be brought in the High Court (Administrative Court – specialist court within the Queen's Bench Division of the High Court of Justice).

The claim will be brought by reference to Part 54 of the civil procedure rules (CPR) and the Home Office guidance on judicial reviews and injunction[2], is normally quite a useful tool to have on

---

1 https://www.judiciary.uk/publications/lord-chief-justices-direction-regarding-the-transfer-of-immigration-and-asylum-judicial-review-cases-to-the-upper-tribunal-immigration-and-asylum-chamber/

2 published on the 10th October 2019 – https://assets.publishing.service.gov.uk/government/uploads/system/uploads/

hand when considering the process in enforcement cases. A claim for judicial review is time limited and must be brought promptly and in any event within three months of the challenged decisions[3]. The Court may on application, extend time at their discretion, but cogent reasons would have to be given for any delay.

Whilst, claims for judicial review, are brought when an individual is in detention, to help secure their release, on the grounds that the detention is unlawful, it may well be that an individual is at the same time also challenging other decisions connected to their immigration history, such as a removal decision. It is important in such cases, to ensure that any challenge to detention being unlawful, is appropriately particularised so that it can be properly ventilated alongside any other issues raised.

The Courts in ***BA and others v SSHD [2012] EWCA Civ 944***[4]and *Ashraf v SSHD [2013] EWHC 4028,*[5] highlighted the potential for an abuse of process in certain circumstances. In ***BA*** the court highlighted where claims for detention were not properly particularised in the judicial review application alongside other challenges such as a challenge to the removal directions and when permission was then refused, a later claim challenging detention in the civil courts could potentially be seen as an abuse. In *Ashraf*, a slightly different approach was taken, with the Court finding if claim to challenge detention was pursued where, there was no 'obvious distinct merit'[6] at the same time as a challenge to removal directions, then this was also open to a finding of abuse. However, each case will have to be considered on its own merit and as long as justifiable reasons are

attachment_data/file/919646/chapter-60-judicial-reviews_v20.0ext.pdf

3 CPR 54.5(1)(a) & (b)

4 *BA and others v SSHD [2012] EWCA Civ 944* at §26-27

5 *Ashraf v SSHD [2013] EWHC 4028* at §28-36

6 ibid §31

given for a certain course of action then individuals and practitioners can protect themselves against any potential sanctions.

These cases clearly demonstrate the need for specialist legal advice in this area of law, in relation to where and how a claim challenging unlawful detention might be taken.

Pre-action Protocol

At the outset of any challenge, the pre-action protocol must be complied with and the CPR on Pre-Action Protocol for Judicial Review[7], highlights relevant matters to be considered in relation to the preparation of such a document. A proforma, which is widely used for immigration cases is also available on the gov.uk website[8]. It is important to keep in mind that a claim for personal injury is to be included then there is a specific Pre-Action Protocol that must also be complied with.

The pre-action protocol should, identify why detention is said to be unlawful, which can only be ascertained after the detention history of an individual is considered. This will include but not limited to:

i. assessing prospects of removal by reference to any barriers such as travel documents etc

ii. considering the paperwork relating to detention and whether reasons given for detention are appropriate

iii. if an individual was detained pending deportation, was the underlying order made lawful (***Draga***)

7 http://www.justice.gov.uk/courts/procedure-rules/civil/protocol/prot_jrv

8 https://www.gov.uk/government/publications/pre-action-protocol-for-judicial-review

iv. considering whether a certain policy is applicable to an individual's circumstances and whether it has been applied appropriately/adequately (***Lumba, Kambadzi***)

v. has there been an adherence with the Rule 34 and Rule 35 process

vi. have appropriate reviews/monthly progress reports been undertaken in detention in accordance with prospect of removal, medical conditions etc.

A subject access request[9] should also be made but this will probably be subject to some delay and may not be made available before proceedings are commenced. Therefore, at this stage of the proceedings it may assist to ask for disclosure of any relevant evidence if necessary, which may include some of the documents highlighted above.

Progressing a Judicial Review application

If a negative response is received or the time given for a response to the pre-action protocol expires, keeping in mind the three-month period in which to bring a claim, an application for permission to apply for judicial review can be brought. Once the claim is lodged in the High Court and served on all parties, it is a matter for the Secretary of State to provide within 21 days an acknowledgment of service together with summary grounds of defence.

The Court considers the application for permission on the papers and if he were to refuse it, renewal grounds can be lodged in order for the matter to be listed before a judge at an oral hearing for per-

9 This is further considered in chapter 7

mission. At this hearing, it is usual for both sides to attend in order to put their case.

If permission is granted then directions will be issued and the matter may then proceed to a full hearing, if the Respondent does not concede prior to this date. Where a consent order is signed at any stage before the full hearing, costs will usually follow, as this is regarded as a win. However, if the matter is refused at an oral hearing, permission can be sought at the same time for onward appeal to the Court of Appeal. This is usually on the basis that the judge, who has refused permission has erred in reasons given for refusing permission. Permission can also be sought directly from the Court of Appeal but such an application, will only be considered on the papers and if not granted, then that is the end of any onward appeals. If the Court of Appeal grants permission on the papers then they would list the matter for a full hearing.

Once the High Court has made a finding that detention was unlawful, then the courts have made clear time and again that the issue of damages should be considered by the civil courts. More recently in the case of ***ZA (Pakistan) v SSHD [2020] EWCA Civ 146*** the court reminded lawyers of the overriding objective which includes the allocation of cases. The court highlighted that "*once the appellant had been released from detention both parties should have addressed their minds to the issue of whether the claim should have been transferred either to the Queen's Bench Division or the County Court*"[10] The next chapter will go on to consider private claims that can be made in the civil courts once an individual is no longer being held in detention and wishes to pursue a claim for damages which includes, a historic period of detention that he claims was unlawful.

10 ***ZA (Pakistan) v SSHD [2020] EWCA Civ 146*** at §72 - 74

Interim Relief

Once an application for judicial review has been made in the High Court challenging unlawful detention, the most pressing concern will be to secure the release of the detainee as the process of judicial review may take some time before there is any finality. The proper course would therefore be to include in any claim by way of injunctive action is, release of the detainee as part of interim relief, which is provided by Section 37 (1)(2) of the Senior Courts Act 1981. This highlights that such relief maybe granted where it appeared that *"it would be just and convenient for the declaration to be made or the injunction to be granted, as the case may be."*[11]

It is quite common for interim relief to be granted where an individual is detained so long as it is in line with the private law principles on interim relief which have been adapted to public law cases, in particular the ***American Cyanamid***[12] test. These guidelines involve an assessment of:

- Whether there is a serious question to be tried
- What would be the balance of convenience of each party, should the order be granted
- Whether there are any special factors adapted to unlawful detention claims, the second point would involve a question of whether damages for unlawful detention would be an adequate remedy for the detained individual.

---

11 S.37(2) of the Senior Courts Act 1981 also see CPR – Part 25 – Interim remedies and security for costs

12 American Cyanamid Co v Ethicom Ltd [1975] AC 396

Looking at the balance of convenience, the course which appears to carry the lowest risk of injustice is the release of a detainee in the event removal was not considered likely in a reasonable period. It is clear where a person is detained then the adequacy of payment of damages is not going to be a sufficient remedy. A very recent example in a case already discussed earlier, where interim relief was being sought was the case of ***R (Detention Action & Anor) v SSHD [2020] EWHC 732 (Admin).***[13] An application for interim relief was made for the release of all detainees, in particular those with pre-existing conditions to the COVID-19 due to the pandemic, but in applying the ***American Cyanamid*** test the application was not successful as, the courts concluded the circumstances created by the COVID-19 pandemic were unprecedented and the Secretary of State's continued actions in response were both 'precautionary and reactive'. Further that the evidence presented had not demonstrated an arguable case that there was a real risk of death or article 3 ill-treatment of persons who remained in detention. The matter did not get beyond the first question, although the balance of convenience was considered in the alternative, with a finding in favour of the Secretary of State.[14]

Inherent jurisdiction to grant bail

It is also useful to keep in mind the High Court has inherent jurisdiction to grant bail[15] in ongoing proceedings and this is often confused by the courts with an application that may have been made for interim relief, in a case.

---

13 ***R (Detention Action & Anor) v SSHD [2020] EWHC 732 (Admin)*** at §17

14 ibid §27-28

15 ***R v Secretary of State for the Home Department ex p Turkoglu*** [1988] 1 QB 398; ***R v Secretary of State for the Home Department ex p Sezek*** [2001] EWCA Civ 795

In the event that interim relief is not granted then an application for bail can be made focusing on principles of bail as discussed above, in particular with reference to whether removal was imminent.

Habeas Corpus

Last but not least on the topic of remedies it is important to remember, Habeas Corpus, which is not now commonly seen in the courts. The process involves an application being made for a writ of Habeas Corpus pursuant to part 87 of the CPR. The translation from Latin for "a writ of Habeas Corpus" is literally to "produce the body" the purpose is to bring before court anyone who alleges/or asserts they are not lawfully being detained. Whilst its roots are founded in common law, it can be used by anyone alleging their detention is not lawful. It has commonly been used by immigration detainees however, given the similarities to judicial review reliance on this in immigration context has waned. At this stage it is important to know the existence of this alternative remedy however, given other effective remedies available for those detained, there is no need for any further detailed discussion.

CHAPTER SEVEN
CIVIL CLAIMS FOR FALSE IMPRISONMENT

Procedure

Keeping in mind the warning given in the case of ***BA and others v SSHD [2012] EWCA Civ 944,*** discussed in the previous chapter, if in an individual does start public law proceedings it is better to include a claim for damages rather than start separate civil proceedings, which would be considered an abuse of process, placing an "*unjust burden on the Secretary of State*". The Home Office will be the party named as defendant in relation to a challenge against detention in the civil courts rather than the Secretary of State who would be the named party in judicial review claims. But there may well be others who are potentially also liable and therefore can included as a party in the action. For example, detention centres run by private companies, may have perpetrated the harm complained.

Where damages are added to the public law proceedings which are then settled in the individual's favour, they are entitled to pursue a claim for damages by way of transferring the proceedings to the Queen's Bench Division or the County Court, who will be better equipped to make the appropriate assessment for damages.

Any claim commenced is usually under Part 7 of the CPR, however, as previously discussed, where a personal injury claim was also being advanced then the relevant protocols under Part 8 of the CPR must also be complied with.

Funding will be an important issue to consider in such claims especially when it comes to making an assessment on what might be recoverable in terms of damages, for e.g. if only nominal damages were available would this satisfy a cost benefit analysis required for the legal aid board if publicly funded.

Limitation periods

In relation to any of the causes of action being pursued consideration must be given to the limitation periods that apply.

i Judicial review – Already highlighted, the CPR at 54.5 requires any claim form must be filed promptly and, in any event, not later than three months after the grounds to make the claim first arose (Although there is some discretion for the court to grant an extension of time).

ii Civil Claims – Such claims are subject a six-year limitation period, therefore if, they do not fall in the three-month limitation period for judicial review proceedings because they may have been released from detention, then the civil proceedings may be more appropriate. This will be considered under the Limitation Act 1980, as an action founded on tort, such that a claim cannot brought after expiration of **six-years** from the date in which the cause of action accrued.[1]

iii Personal injury claims – This is also governed by the Limitation Act 1980, in particular Section 11, which limits a period applicable to three years from either the date on which the cause of action accrued or the date of knowledge (if later when the person was injured).[2]

1 s.2 of the Limitation Act 1980

2 s.11(4) of the Limitation Act 1980

iv Human Rights claims – The limitation period for a Human Rights claim in one-year from the date of the act complained of, pursuant to Section 7(5) of the Human rights Act 1998.

Whilst, these limitation periods are clearly stipulated in statute an extension may be requested on a discretionary basis, however there would need to be cogent reasons as to why an extension ought to be granted.

Pre-action Considerations

A similar analysis of an individual's detention history is required, as has been highlighted in the previous chapter, which will help identify the period of detention that is said to be unlawful. This is a vital pre-action consideration and at this stage it is also appropriate to consider the heads of damages and likely quantum available by way of a comparison to other similar cases in which quantum has been awarded (refer to Appendix A – Table of Cases Relating to Quantum)

In historic claims for unlawful detention, the first step will be gathering the information required, this will usually be by way of making a subject access request under the Data Protection Act 1998. You must apply using an online application form[3] making a detailed request for all documents, held by the Home Office, which should include records from time of entry into the UK through to immigration, asylum and detention records.

The records will contain authorisations/reasons for detention, detention reviews, detention minutes, monthly progress reports and copies of any entries on the GCID (General cases information

3 https://visas-immigration.service.gov.uk/product/saru

database)[4]. A timeline can then be constructed also considering evidence the detainee's representative may have by way of their own records, where they contacted the Home Office, submitted medical records or when they may have flagged medical conditions to the detention officials. Further evidence may also need to be obtained, for example, medical evidence relating to pre-existing conditions and how they have been affected by detention.

It would also be useful to obtain advice as to the strengths of a claim, possible heads of damages, likely quantum, limitation period, potential defendants, whether any parties to the claims should be anonymised as well as, whether further disclosure of particular evidence that may be required specific to an individual's case.

In relation to the format of the letter before claim, it must contain the following key factors:

- Background and all relevant factors;
- Period of detention said to be unlawful;
- The relevant legal framework, which governs at individual's detention (refer to the IS91R and IS91 the document containing the reasons for detention and authority to detain respectively);
- Submissions on applicability of the law;
- The level of damages sought

4 This database began in 2000 and is a record of after-entry operational and case working actions including; personal data outcomes of applications notes taken as part of the decision making process

- Any actions the defendant is expected to take (for example acceptance of liability and damages sought);

- Consideration of any Alternative Dispute Resolution (ADR) proposals;

- Disclosure for any further evidence which the Home Office may be relying on as justifying detention

- Time in which a response is expected – the more complex a case the longer the period given to Home Office, which can range from fourteen days through to four months, however, where time is of the essence and the limitation period is approaching, then this ought to be highlighted to ensure that a claim can be lodged in order to protect an individual's position, especially where it is not possible for the defendant to provide a response within the short period allowed.

Issuing a Claim

The value of any claim, together with the complexity will determine where it ought to be brought. In particular claims in excess of £100,000, or if below £100,000 but complex in nature, ought to be pursued in the High Court.[5] Once the claim is issued by the court, the claim form must be served on the defendant within four months.[6] The particulars of claim should also be served with the claim form, or within fourteen days after service of the claim form[7] and in any event no later than expiration of the claim form.[8]

---

5 CPR (Practice Direction) PD7A §2.1 & PD29 §2.2 (c) & 2.6

6 CPR r7.5(1)

7 CPR r7.4(1)

8 CPR r7.4(2)

It is important for those not familiar with the civil procedure rules to ensure they are complying with the timetable in place for managing each stage of the proceedings, to avoid any sanctions. There is also an obligation on parties to comply with cost management procedures by filing and exchanging budgets setting out their estimated costs for each stage in the proceedings. This is a very important part of the civil proceedings, as the aim is to save time and costs involved for all parties and if not done in a timely manner can lead to there being no consideration of a party's cost budget unless they applied for relief of sanctions[9].

Part 36 Offers

A Part 36 offer is a valuable strategic consideration which can be made at any time (including prior to commencement of proceedings) but it should be made on the proscribed form or in accordance with CPR r36.5.

Many unlawful detention claims are settled, after pre-action stage and if an offer made is lower than what was anticipated, there is always room for negotiation. Settlement at this stage must be considered in light of a number of factors, most important with an eye on the litigation risk in relation to costs, as well as a duty to the legal aid provider and also importantly an individual's position in relation to being able to actually effectively pursue their claim (for example, where a claimant may be a vulnerable and risk of being re-traumatised).

9 This calls for a three-stage test to be satisfied, set out in ***Denton and Others v TH White Limited and Others [2014] EWCA Civ 906***

The acceptance or rejection of Part 36 claim does have cost consequences, therefore any offer made should be carefully considered with reference to CPR Rule 36.[10]

10 CPR 36.17 (4)(a) – see case of ***Mohammed v The Home Office [2017] EWHC 3051 (QB) (24 November 2017)***

CHAPTER EIGHT
DAMAGES

This is an important chapter for anyone bringing a claim for unlawful detention, as it is important to assessing the overall merit of bringing an action, in particular in civil courts, for those individuals who are no longer in detention.

In the first instance, considering whether an individual would have been lawfully detained requires an assessment in accordance with the ordinary civil standard of proof, that is a balance of probabilities[1] with the burden of proof on the Secretary of State.[2]

Once liability has been established by a finding that an individual was unlawfully detained, the next step is an assessment of what loss was suffered by the individual. This is because whilst, false imprisonment is a strict liability tort, individuals may not be able to demonstrate an actual loss. Therefore on one hand, the Courts may accept detention was unlawful, but they may not go on to award substantial damages. This is discussed in further detail below.

Types of Damages

There are seven identifiable heads of loss and these can further be categorised in three groups as follows:

---

1 OM (Nigeria) v SSHD [2011] EWCA Civ 909 paragraph 23

2 R (EO) v SSHD [2013] EWHC 1236 (Admin) paragraph 70-74

i **Nominal Damages**

- Nominal damages – for claims where there is no identifiable loss

ii **Compensatory Damages**

- Basic/General damages/Loss of Liberty – awarded for the actual time spent unlawfully detained
- Aggravated damages – where the defendant's conduct justifies a greater award
- Personal injury – where there has been pain, suffering and loss of amenity in causing or contributing/exacerbating a medical condition
- Special damages – specific pecuniary loss; loss of earnings, medical costs etc
- Just satisfaction for breach of Human Rights Act 1998

iii **Punitive Damages**

- Exemplary damages – punitive to express disapproval of the defendant's conduct

The Appendix to this guide, will set out cases, where damages have been awarded, identifying the relevant elements. Case law is limited on quantum as often, damages may be settled once a finding of unlawful detention is made and/or it may be transferred to the civil courts, which makes it difficult to track the amount awarded in such cases.

Nominal Damages

Nominal damages are awarded to individuals who would and could have been lawfully detained in any event. The case of ***Lumba (WL) v*** *SSHD [2011] UKSC 12* highlighted at paragraph 95:

> *The question here is simply whether, on the hypothesis under consideration, the victims of the false imprisonment have suffered any loss which should be compensated in more than nominal damages. Exemplary damages apart, the purpose of damages is to compensate the victims of civil wrongs for the loss and damage that the wrongs have caused. If the power to detain had been exercised by the application of lawful policies, and on the assumption that the Hardial Singh principles had been properly applied (an issue which I discuss at paras 129-148 below), it is inevitable that the appellants would have been detained. In short, they suffered no loss or damage as a result of the unlawful exercise of the power to detain. They should receive no more than nominal damages.*

A recent example of an award of nominal damages was seen in the case of ***R (Aboro) v Secretary of State for the Home Department*** **[2018] EWHC 1436 (Admin)**, where the challenge to detention was on the basis of a failure to consider medical evidence, namely a psychiatric report. It was held that the Secretary of State had failed to comply with its duties under Chapter 55 (Detention and Temporary Release) of the UKBA Enforcement Instructions and Guidance (EIG)[3] which sanctions detention of "*those suffering serious mental illness which cannot be satisfactorily managed within detention*" in "*very*

3 Now replaced with Chapter 55, discussed earlier

exceptional circumstances". However, despite detention being procedurally flawed with public law errors, as there was a failure to consider a relevant policy, the Claimant was only entitled to nominal damages as his condition was being managed in detention as per evidence from the doctor he had seen in detention. It was held therefore even if the relevant policy had been considered he would nevertheless have been detained.

The court further found there to be no breach of *Hardial Singh* principles, and additionally that any claim under Article 3 of the ECHR was unarguable.

Basic /General Damages

i General principles

An assessment is made for damages is on a case by case basis and the mechanical calculation on a daily rate has been discouraged time and again. Guidance was given on the correct approach in the case of ***R (on the application of Evans) v Governor HM Prison Brockhill [1998] EWCA Civ 1042, [1999] 1 QB 1043 at 1060***. It was highlighted that a "*global approach*" was used to ensure that the calculation focused on the following elements:

- Compensation of loss and liberty and;
- Damage to reputation, humiliation, shock (where not previously detained), injury to feelings which are as a result of loss of liberty.

- Damages which are evidenced in relation to psychiatric or physical injury[4]

The key authority in relation to the principles for assessing damages is ***Thompson v. Commissioner of Police for the Metropolis [1998] QB 498*** and in the case of ***MK (Algeria) v Secretary of State for the Home Department [2010] EWCA Civ 980*** at para 8, per Laws LJ[5] distils the important principles from the guidance given in the case of ***Thompson and Hsu*** as follows:

> *"There are three general principles which should be born in mind: 1) the assessment of damages should be sensitive to the facts and the particular case and the degree of harm suffered by the particular claimant: see the leading case of Thompson v Commissioner of Police [1998] QB 498 at 515A and also the discussion at page 1060 in R v Governor of Brockhill Prison Ex Parte Evans [1999] QB 1043; 2) Damages should not be assessed mechanistically as by fixing a rigid figure to be awarded for each day of incarceration: see Thompson at 516A. A global approach should be taken: see Evans 1060 E; 3) While obviously the gravity of a false imprisonment is worsened by its length the amount broadly attributable to the increasing passage of time should be tapered or placed on a reducing scale. This is for two reasons: (i) to keep this class of damages in proportion with those payable in personal injury and perhaps other cases; and (ii) because the initial shock of being detained will generally attract a higher rate of compensation than the detention's continuance: Thompson 515 E-F.*

4 In relation to any elements of personal injury being claimed the Judicial College Guidelines would also be a useful source to consult

5 These principles were further endorsed in the cases of: ***KG v Secretary of State for the Home Department [2018] EWHC 3665 (Admin),*** para 30*;* ***Diop v Secretary of State for the Home Department [2018] EWHC 3420 (Admin),*** para 28, ***and Majewski v Secretary of State for the Home Department [2019] EWHC 473 (Admin),*** para 11.

Therefore the focus is clearly on three key issues:

- A fact sensitive assessment
- Any assessment should be a "global approach" not mechanistic or rigid by reference to a daily rate
- Where detention involves a lengthy period, then damages should be tapered to ensure the assessment is proportionate to other awards e.g. personal injury awards and in any case initial shock award would attract a higher award at outset of detention.

Initial Shock

An important issue, to consider in the first instance is whether or not the detainee is entitled to compensation for the "initial shock" of detention, that is, considering whether, he was someone who had been previously detained either in immigration detention or in prison due to criminal offending and was then transferred into immigration detention.

Quite helpfully the Court of Appeal in ***MK***, also isolated the starting point for an amount someone would be entitled to for the first hour and then the initial twenty four hours of detention, which certainly makes calculating damages in such a claim slightly easier. This was set as follows:

> *9 In Thompson the court gave specific guidance (515 D-F) to the effect that in a "straightforward case of wrongful arrest and imprisonment" the starting point was likely to be about £500 for the first hour of loss of liberty and a claimant wrongly detained for 24 hours should for that alone normally be entitled to an award of*

> *about £3,000. That case was of course decided more than ten years ago and, while not forgetting the imperative that damages should not be assessed mechanistically, some uplift to these starting points would plainly be appropriate to take account of inflation. Mr Singh for the respondent Secretary of State before us commends in particular the decision of Mr Kenneth Parker QC, as he then was, in Beecroft v SSHD [2008] EWHC Admin 3189. That is a helpful decision. It is very different on the facts from the case before us and it is right to say, as indeed Thompson itself makes clear, all these cases are fact-sensitive.*

Inflation and Uplift

It is also important to ensure, when estimating the level of damages in your case by reference to a previous awards, that care is taken to ensure the award is adjusted for inflation, as well as in accordance with the principles in ***Simmons v Castle [2012] EWCA Civ 1288***[6], which held that for general damages, awards preceding that decision (1st April 2013) should be uplifted by 10% when used as precedents.

At today's date, (October 2020) if the amounts estimated in ***Thompson*** (February 1997) were adjusted for inflation and a 10% uplift was added, an individual would be entitled to the following awards:

6 This judgement reflects the loss of a "success fee" after the *Jackson* reforms to civil litigation in 2013

AWARD DATE	Thompson (February 1997)	October 2020 (10% uplift)
First Hour	£500	£1051.60
First 24 Hours	£3000	£6,308.50

Aggravated Damages

One can draw further guidance from the case of ***Thompson*** when assessing whether an award of aggravated damages is could be made as follows:

> *"Such damages can be awarded where there are aggravating features about the case which would result in the plaintiff not receiving sufficient compensation for the injury suffered if the award were restricted to a basic award. Aggravating features can include humiliating circumstances at the time of arrest or any conduct of those responsible for the arrest or the prosecution which shows that they had behaved in a high handed, insulting, malicious or oppressive manner either in relation to the arrest or imprisonment or in conducting the prosecution. Aggravating features can also include the way the litigation and trial are conducted."*[7]

Therefore factors to look out for when making an assessment of whether there is a valid claim for aggravated damages are:

- humiliating circumstances at the time of the arrest,
- conduct of those responsible for the arrest

7 ***Thompson*** per Lord Woolf at 516B-C

- the way the litigation and trial were conducted.

The case of ***Thompson*** also held that if there were to be an award of aggravating damages, the award it was unlikely to be less than £1,000, nor were they likely to be twice the basic damages except perhaps where, on the particular facts, the basic damages are modest. The relevant part of that judgment is as follows:

> *(10) We consider that where it is appropriate to award aggravated damages the figure is unlikely to be less than a £1,000. We do not think it is possible to indicate a precise arithmetical relationship between basic damages and aggravated damages because the circumstances will vary from case to case. In the ordinary way, however, we would not expect the aggravated damages to be as much as twice the basic damages except perhaps where, on the particular facts, the basic damages are modest.*
>
> *(11) It should be strongly emphasised to the jury that the total figure for basic and aggravated damages should not exceed what they consider is fair compensation for the injury which the plaintiff has suffered. It should also be explained that if aggravated damages are awarded such damages, though compensatory are not intended as a punishment, will in fact contain a penal element as far as the defendant is concerned.* [8]

It is of note in considering further guidance in ***Thompson*** that an award of aggravated damages already compensates for any injury an individual suffers as a result of oppressive and insulting behaviour when they're detained, such that it should then not be double counted as exemplary damages.

---

8 ***Thompson*** per Lord Woolf at 516D-G §10-§11

Special Damages

This is factual financial loss, not commonly seen in claims for unlawful detention, however, it is recoverable, if it is caused as a direct result of the unlawful detention. The specifics must be added to the claim and may well include damaged property, loss of earnings, where an individual had permission to work or even medical bills.

Exemplary Damages

These kind of damages are less common in immigration detention cases, than aggravated damages as per the guidance of ***Thompson*** such damages would be to punish those cases where:

- *"there has been conduct, including oppressive or arbitrary behaviour, by police officers which deserves the exceptional remedy of exemplary damages"* [9]
- other damages awarded are "*inadequate to punish him for his outrageous conduct, to mark their disapproval of such conduct and to deter him from repeating it*" [10]
- an important consideration for anyone looking at awarding such damages was that this would be considered a *"windfall"* and was being paid from public funds.[11]
- such damages would only be awarded to mark disapproval of the oppressive or arbitrary behaviour.[12]

9 ***Thompson*** per Lord Woolf at 516H-517A – §12(a)
10 ***Thompson*** per Lord Woolf at 516H-517A – §12(b)
11 ***Thompson*** per Lord Woolf at P517B – §12(c)
12 ***Thompson*** per Lord Woolf at P517A – §12(d)

In ***Thompson*** it was said that where exemplary damages were appropriate, they were unlikely to be less than £5000 at the very least an award of £25,000, where there had been behaviour which was particularly deserving of condemnation involving high ranking officers, with a maximum award of up to £50,000.[13]

When making a claim for damages, it is also important to look at the conduct of the detainee as it was held that any improper conduct could reduce or even eliminate any award for aggravated or exemplary damages, if he has contributed to the behaviour complained of.[14]

Personal Injury

This includes damages for pain, suffering and loss of amenity in exacerbating a medical condition and can be calculated by reference to the judicial college guidelines for the assessment of general damages in personal injury cases.

Just Satisfaction for a breach under the Human Rights Act 1998

Proceedings are brought with reference to section 7 of the Human Rights Act 1998, where there have been breaches of a convention rights, section 8 of the Act empowers the courts to award damages or order a payment of compensation in civil proceedings. There are three routes under the European Convention of Human Rights (ECHR) through which damages may be sought and awarded:

- Article 5 – damages are very likely to overlap with those available for unlawful detention. Careful consideration will

13 ***Thompson*** per Lord Woolf at P517C-D – §13

14 ***Thompson*** per Lord Woolf at P517D-E – §14

need to be given to which element of Article 5 is being relied on to demonstrate a breach of the Convention Rights. It is important to note that if there is an argument that domestic primary legislation required detention which was contrary to a convention right, then only the European Court of Human Rights (ECtHR) would be in the position to award damages.

- Article 3 – this commonly relates to an award of damages where there is an impact on individuals who suffer mental health issues as a result of detention. An individual would have to demonstrate that the detention violated their rights under Article 3 of the ECHR, which prohibits torture or/and inhuman or degrading treatment or punishment.

- Article 8 of the ECHR – this is uncommon and relates to claims for damages to cover cases where there has been an unjustified separation of family.

APPENDIX
TABLE OF CASES RELATING TO QUANTUM

CASE NAME	TIME	FACTS RELEVANT TO QUANTUM	BASIC DAMAGES	OTHER DAMAGES	TOTAL	RELEVANT DATE FOR QUANTUM (USED FOR INFLATION & UPLIFT ON CASES PRE 01/04/2003)
R (on the application of E) v SSHD [2006] EWHC 2500 (Admin)	2–3 days	Detained in the early hours and unlawfully removed to Iran. He had previous good character	**Interim award** of **£4000** based on **£6000** at trial.	**(i)Shock of arrest award**		25/07/2006
R (on the application of B) v SSHD [2008] EWHC 3189 (Admin)	6 months	Victim of torture – Detained in breach Detention Centre Rules and policies on detention of victims of torture.	**£32,000**	**(i) Aggravated** – no due diligence by the SSHD and unjustified defence maintained to the end – **£6,000** **(ii) No shock of arrest award**	**£38,000**	04/12/2008
Muuse: EWHC 1886 (QB); [2010] EWCA Civ 453	128 days	Dutch national detained pending deportation to Somalia despite evidence of his Dutch nationality being available.	**£25,000**	**(i) Aggravated** – Defendant's conduct worthy of punishment – **£7,500** **(ii) Exemplary** – Treated in "high handed" and "oppressive" manner – **£27,500** **(iii) No shock of arrest** – previously imprisoned	**£60,000**	13/07/2009
R (on the application of Mehari) v SSHD [2010] EWHC 636 (Admin)	7 days	Unlawful detention followed by a period of lawful detention for just over 2 months. Good character, distress of detention were relevant factors.	**£4,000**	**(i) Shock of arrest award**	**£4,000**	22/02/2010

MK (Algeria) v SSHD [2010] EWCA Civ 980	24 days	Algerian national married to EEA national detained on basis that he had failed to respond to further request for evidence that wife no longer exercising Treaty rights. No proper enquiries made by the Defendant.	**£12,500**	(i) **Aggravated** – Defendant's acted in a "blinkered and high-handed manner" **£5,000;** **(ii) Shock of arrest award**	£17,500	29/04/2010
R (on the application of J) v SSHD [2011] EWHC 3073 (Admin)	4 days	Defendant relied on procedurally flawed age assessment and treated J as an adult Basic damages reflected fact that J was detained as adult not a child	£7,500	(i) **Aggravated damages** – Defendants were "high-handed and unnecessarily aggressive treatment" i.e. use of handcuffs – **£2,500** (ii) **Shock of arrest award**	**£10,000**	24/11/2011
R (on the application of M) v SSHD [2011] EWHC 3667 (Admin)	Less than 24 hours	Family was unlawfully removed from the UK, without notice. Damages awarded and adjusted in light of the return of family being ordered.	**@£2,500 (£5000)**- father and son; **@£3,000 (£9,000)**- mother and daughters.	(i) **Aggravated: @£2,000** (£4,000) to father & son(over18); **@£3,000** (£9,000) to mother (mental health issues) and two daughters (under 18). **ii) Special** – **£10,000** loss of property. **(iii) Shock of arrest** - (especially given time and manner of detention)	**£37,000**	06/12/2011
R (on the application of NAB) v. SSHD [2011] EWHC 1191 (Admin)	82 days	Iranian national refused to sign the documents which the Iranian authorities held to be necessary. NAB chose detention in UK over freedom in Iran. Inactivity of the Defendant, whilst, NAB was detained with no reasonable prospect of removal rendered that period of detention, unlawful.	**£6,150** (working on daily rate of £75)	(i) **No shock of arrest award**	**£6,150**	13/05/2011

R (on the application of Bent) v SSHD [2012] EWHC 4036 (Admin)	23 days	Detention became unlawful once removal directions quashed given B's further representations on Art 8, which would lead to an in-country appeal right if refused. Damages accounted for effect on well-being.	**£12,500**	(i) **No shock of arrest award** as he was lawfully detained for the first 14 days	**£12,500**	28/09/2012
R (on the application of Shaw) v SSHD [2013] EWHC 42 (Admin)	10 hours	Failure to allow a mother and son any time to seek legal advice after they were served with removal directions. Removal as a result was unlawful the period whilst that removal was effected was unlawful, including time spent on flight.	**@£2,000 each** (**£4000**) – mother and son	(i) On facts of case **no aggravated or exemplary** damages (ii) **No shock of arrest award**	**£4,000**	18/01/2013
R (on the application of AS) v SSHD 2015 EWHC 1331 (QB)	61 days	As a child detained on basis of flawed assessment of age. Relevant factors: detention 25% responsible for the adjustment disorder symptoms and 50% PTSD	**£23,000**	(i) **Aggravated damages** – no understanding of process, Defendant not apologise before trial despite accepting unlawfully detained – **£5000;** (ii) **Personal injury** – Shock – **£3500**	**£31,500**	13/05/2015
NS v SSHD [2013] CSOH 139, [2014] CSIH 91	362 days	NS was detained pending enquiries as to her nationality. Detention became unlawful when removal was no longer imminent and there was a low risk of offending.	**£36,000 (inclusive of interest)**	(i) **No shock of arrest award** as was lawfully detained for 7 moths previously	**£36,000**	21/08/2013

R (on the application of Lamari) v SSHD [2013] EWHC 3130 (QB)	23 days	Detained subject to deportation order, however L, challenged the lawfulness of his continued immigration detention. Court ordered release given effect on L's mental health of continuing detention. Defendant gave an undertaking to release within 14 days of hearing of JR but then, in contempt of court, failed to release for further 6 days. Basic damages took in to account serious mental health problems of L	£10,000	(i) **Aggravated damages** – conduct in releasing him late at night and without proper arrangements such that he had to sleep outside the bail hostel – **£5,000** (ii) **Exemplary damages** – egregious conduct, found to be in contempt of court given breach of undertaking **£10,000** (iii) **Shock of arrest award** from the moment he should have been released	£25,000	16/10/2013
R (on the application of Supawan) v SSHD [2014] EWHC 3224 (Admin)	14 days	The Defendant should have taken into account that the S had a pending judicial review claim.	£9,000	(i) **No shock of arrest award** as initial arrest was lawful	£9,000	05/06/2014
R (on the application of Palisetty) v Home Office [2014] EWHC 2473 (QB)	17.5 hours	Detained on re-entry due to there being a change of circumstances, to Tier 4 visa. The court held the period pending removal was unlawful. P was also entitled to recover special damages: flight from London to Hyderabad	£3,509.48 (in accordance with the first 24 hours rate in *Thompson*)	(i) **Special damages** – **£624.93** – (travel expenses); (ii) **No shock of arrest**	£4,134.41	21/07/2014
R (on the application of Santos) v SSHD [2016] EWHC 609 (Admin)	154 days	S, a Brazilian national applied as a spouse of an EEA national. S was arrested and detained despite no decision being made on the residence card application, though. Relevant facts include, delay of nearly 4 years in issuing a residence card, repeated attempts to remove him during that time, lost earnings because employers were misinformed of his status, a ruined credit history, permanent disruption to family relationships and friendships and very	£40,000	(i) **Aggravated damages** – disregarded explanation of S about his legitimate status in under EEA law. Further treatment at Colnbrook was degrading- **£10,000;** (ii) **Exemplary damages** – Defendant's behaviour outrageous, oppressive and unconstitution al they had	£76,578 **(with damages for breach of EU Law total – £136,048)**	23/03/2016

		considerable distress.		failed to give full and accurate information to the court -**£20,000;** **(iii) Loss of earning – £6,578** **(iv) Shock of arrest award** **(v) (Separately for Breach of EU law – £59,470)**		
R (on the application of AXD) v. Home Office [2016] EWHC 1617 (QB)	614 days	AXD served a prison sentence and was then held in immigration detention pending deportation. Initial period of 16 months was lawful followed but court held given delays in further action by the Defendant the risk to the public, and of absconding, was not so great that continued incarceration was the only real option.	**£80,000**	**(i) Aggravated damages –** serious delays to decision making, received sub-optimal treatment for his schizophrenia, released with no welfare plan, failure in the Defendant's duty of candour – **£25,000;** **(ii) No shock of arrest award** – previously detained in prison.	**£105,000**	05/07/2016
R (on the application of Chaprazada) v SSHD [2017] EWHC 1209 (Admin)	70 days	Zimbabwean national was detained, however, Defendant's failure to serve the notice of decision refusing a variation application for leave to remain rendered detention unlawful and a later asylum decision supplemented rather than supplanted decision.	**£7,000**	Shock of arrest award for the first 24 hours – **£3,500** (formed part of basic award)	**£7,000**	24/05/2017
R (on the application of Belfken) v SSHD [2017] EWHC 1834 (Admin)	295 days	Moroccan national detained pending deportation. It was held no reasonable prospect of removal given failure to secure ETD on five occasions. Substantial damages awarded for the whole period (despite B's conduct in obstructing the Defendant's efforts to secure removal).	**£40,000**	**(i) No aggravated damages** **(ii) No shock of arrest award**		19/07/2017

Sino v SSHD [2017] EWCA Civ 1975	150 days	Unlawful detention pending deportation where the damages were awarded for procedural unfairness only. See ***Sino, R (on the application of) v Secretary of State for the Home Department*** [2016] EWHC 803 (Admin) (12 April 2016)	**£3,750** (originally awarded by the High Court now remitted on appeal for further assessment)			31/10/2017
R (on the application of Mohammed) v SSHD [2017] EWHC 2809 (QB)	445 days	M, a prolific and violent offender detained unlawfully for three periods of detention of 41 days in 2012, 139 days in 2013, and 265 days in 2015-2016 under immigration powers. Deportation within a reasonable period was remote, further M was a victim of torture and PTSD sufferer and the court found breaches of rule 35 procedure with the Defendant maintaining an unmeritorious defence until the eve of the hearing (aggravating features). The court also considered that the prison was more restrictive environment than the Immigration Removal centre and M had spent 260 days in prison.	**£78,500** (£8,500-41days; £25,000-139days £45,000-265days)	(i) **No shock of arrest award** (as previously in prison)	**£78,500**	08/11/2017

R (on the application of Sapkota) v SSHD [2017] EWHC 2857 (Admin)	36 days	Immigration Officer wrongfully decided S was attempting to extend his leave to remain by entering into a bigamous marriage. Aggravating features of detention: - he was held for hours without heating and without adequate food or drink; - he was accused of bigamy in front of his fiancée with no real opportunity to rebut the allegation; - he was told of his curtailment of leave and immediate detention in a "causal and callous way"; and - his "shock, embarrassment and distress" was increased by the fact he had never been arrested or detained before	For the first 24 hours – **£6,000;** Remaining 35 days: **£12,000** **(£18,000)**	(i) **Aggravated damages** for the first 24 hours – **£5,000;** (ii) **Special damages** – loss of earnings – **£658.63** (iii) **Shock of Arrest award**	**£23,658.63**	13/11/2017
Jollah, R (On the Application Of) v Secretary of State for the Home Department (No. 2) [2017] EWHC 2821	2.5 years (curfew)	Concession that curfew requirement was unlawful as could only be attached as a condition of bail. Relevant factor: not detained or subject to restraint, was restricted to his residential address, there was no initial shock (Upheld in the Court of Appeal in ***R (on the application of Jollah) v Secretary of State for the Home Department [2018] EWCA Civ 1260*** and Supreme Court in **R (on the application of Jalloh (formerly Jollah) v SSHD [2020] UKSC 4**, dismissed Defendant's further appeal)	**£4,000**	(i) **No Aggravated damages**	**£4,000**	09/11/2017
R (KG on the application of) v SSHD [2018] EWHC 3665 (Admin)	30 days	Sri Lankan national detained in breach of Detention Centre Rule 34, and the requirement for medical examination within 24 hours of his admission. Relevant factors: vulnerable and mental health exacerbated by detention, previous good character.	**£17,500**	(i) **Aggravated damages** -to protect those where independent evidence of torture exists – **£2,000**	**£19,500**	16/11/2018

R (on the application of Diop) v SSHD [2018] EWHC 1934	28 days	Defendant was not acting lawfully in administering the section 4 bail accommodation after D was granted bail in principle. This resulted in D being unlawfully detained following the initial lawful detention. Relevant factors: D had no knowledge that he had been deprived of his liberty and initially relieved he would not be released until accommodation was arranged.	**£9,000**	(i) No justification to divide basic and aggravated damages **(ii) No shock of arrest award** (as already in prison)	**£9,000**	13/12/2018
R (on the application of Majewski) v SSHD [2019] EWHC 473 (Admin)	38 days	An EEA national was unlawfully detained in the course of Operation Gopik, the Home Office enforcement operation to detain EEA nationals found sleeping rough. Following judgement *Gureckis*, the Defendant conceded M was unlawfully detained as the policy was found to be unlawful and an abuse of rights under r.26 Immigration (EEA) Regulations 2016	**£14,800** (**£6,400** for the **initial shock** and first 24 hours of detention; and **£8,400** for the remaining 37 days)	**(i) No aggravated or exemplary damages** (no particular features warranted this including alcohol dependency) **(ii) No shock of arrest award**	**£14,800**	01/03/2019
R (on the application of Holownia) v SSHD [2019] EWHC 794 (Admin)	153 days	H, a Polish national was detained sleeping rough at his workplace. Following judgement *Gureckis*, the Defendant conceded H was unlawfully detained as above. His partial hunger strike was considered as a relevant. Damages for psychiatric injury remained outstanding	**£32,000 (£6,000** for **initial shock)**	**(i) Aggravated damages** (hunger strike) **£5,000;** **(ii) Shock of arrest award – £6,000;**	**£37,000**	03/04/2019
R (on the application of Deptka and anor) v SSHD [2019] EWHC 503 (Admin)	154 days	Polish couple sleeping rough were detained and following judgement *Gureckis*, the Defendant conceded they were unlawfully detained as above. Relevant factors: despite previous convictions this was first detention	**@£35,000 each** (**@£5,000** each for **initial shock**)	**(i) Aggravated damages - £8,500** each (couple were separated for 4 weeks and undue delay if Defendant admitting liability or offering apology). **(ii) Shock of arrest award – £5,000;**	**£87,000**	18/01/2019

MORE BOOKS BY LAW BRIEF PUBLISHING

A selection of our other titles available now:-

'A Practical Guide to the Pre-Action RTA Claims Protocol for Personal Injury Lawyers' by Antonia Ford
'A Practical Guide to Neighbour Disputes and the Law' by Alexander Walsh
'A Practical Guide to Forfeiture of Leases' by Mark Shelton
'A Practical Guide to Coercive Control for Legal Practitioners and Victims' by Rachel Horman
'A Practical Guide to Rights Over Airspace and Subsoil' by Daniel Gatty
'Tackling Disclosure in the Criminal Courts – A Practitioner's Guide' by Narita Bahra QC & Don Ramble
'A Practical Guide to the Law of Driverless Cars – Second Edition' by Alex Glassbrook, Emma Northey & Scarlett Milligan
'A Practical Guide to TOLATA Claims' by Greg Williams
'Artificial Intelligence – The Practical Legal Issues' by John Buyers
'A Practical Guide to the Law of Prescription in Scotland' by Andrew Foyle
'A Practical Guide to the Construction and Rectification of Wills and Trust Instruments' by Edward Hewitt
'A Practical Guide to the Law of Bullying and Harassment in the Workplace' by Philip Hyland
'How to Be a Freelance Solicitor: A Practical Guide to the SRA-Regulated Freelance Solicitor Model' by Paul Bennett
'A Practical Guide to Prison Injury Claims' by Malcolm Johnson
'A Practical Guide to the Small Claims Track' by Dominic Bright
'A Practical Guide to Advising Clients at the Police Station' by Colin Stephen McKeown-Beaumont
'A Practical Guide to Antisocial Behaviour Injunctions' by Iain Wightwick
'Practical Mediation: A Guide for Mediators, Advocates, Advisers, Lawyers, and Students in Civil, Commercial, Business, Property, Workplace, and Employment Cases' by Jonathan Dingle with John Sephton
'The Mini-Pupillage Workbook' by David Boyle

'A Practical Guide to Crofting Law' by Brian Inkster
'A Practical Guide to Spousal Maintenance' by Liz Cowell
'A Practical Guide to the Law of Domain Names and Cybersquatting' by Andrew Clemson
'A Practical Guide to the Law of Gender Pay Gap Reporting' by Harini Iyengar
'A Practical Guide to the Rights of Grandparents in Children Proceedings' by Stuart Barlow
'NHS Whistleblowing and the Law' by Joseph England
'Employment Law and the Gig Economy' by Nigel Mackay & Annie Powell
'A Practical Guide to Noise Induced Hearing Loss (NIHL) Claims' by Andrew Mckie, Ian Skeate, Gareth McAloon
'An Introduction to Beauty Negligence Claims – A Practical Guide for the Personal Injury Practitioner' by Greg Almond
'Intercompany Agreements for Transfer Pricing Compliance' by Paul Sutton
'Zen and the Art of Mediation' by Martin Plowman
'A Practical Guide to the SRA Principles, Individual and Law Firm Codes of Conduct 2019 – What Every Law Firm Needs to Know' by Paul Bennett
'A Practical Guide to Adoption for Family Lawyers' by Graham Pegg
'A Practical Guide to Industrial Disease Claims' by Andrew Mckie & Ian Skeate
'A Practical Guide to Redundancy' by Philip Hyland
'A Practical Guide to Vicarious Liability' by Mariel Irvine
'A Practical Guide to Applications for Landlord's Consent and Variation of Leases' by Mark Shelton
'A Practical Guide to Relief from Sanctions Post-Mitchell and Denton' by Peter Causton
'A Practical Guide to Equity Release for Advisors' by Paul Sams
'A Practical Guide to Unlawful Eviction and Harassment' by Stephanie Lovegrove
'A Practical Guide to the Law Relating to Food' by Ian Thomas

'A Practical Guide to Financial Services Claims' by Chris Hegarty
'The Law of Houses in Multiple Occupation: A Practical Guide to HMO Proceedings' by Julian Hunt
'A Practical Guide to Unlawful Eviction and Harassment' by Stephanie Lovegrove
'A Practical Guide to Solicitor and Client Costs' by Robin Dunne
'Occupiers, Highways and Defective Premises Claims: A Practical Guide Post-Jackson – 2nd Edition' by Andrew Mckie
'A Practical Guide to Financial Ombudsman Service Claims' by Adam Temple & Robert Scrivenor
'A Practical Guide to Advising Schools on Employment Law' by Jonathan Holden
'A Practical Guide to Running Housing Disrepair and Cavity Wall Claims: 2nd Edition' by Andrew Mckie & Ian Skeate
'A Practical Guide to Holiday Sickness Claims – 2nd Edition' by Andrew Mckie & Ian Skeate
'Arguments and Tactics for Personal Injury and Clinical Negligence Claims' by Dorian Williams
'A Practical Guide to QOCS and Fundamental Dishonesty' by James Bentley
'A Practical Guide to Drone Law' by Rufus Ballaster, Andrew Firman, Eleanor Clot
'A Practical Guide to Compliance for Personal Injury Firms Working With Claims Management Companies' by Paul Bennett
'A Practical Guide to the Landlord and Tenant Act 1954: Commercial Tenancies' by Richard Hayes & David Sawtell
'A Practical Guide to Dog Law for Owners and Others' by Andrea Pitt
'RTA Allegations of Fraud in a Post-Jackson Era: The Handbook – 2nd Edition' by Andrew Mckie
'RTA Personal Injury Claims: A Practical Guide Post-Jackson' by Andrew Mckie
'On Experts: CPR35 for Lawyers and Experts' by David Boyle
'An Introduction to Personal Injury Law' by David Boyle

'A Practical Guide to Chronic Pain Claims' by Pankaj Madan
'A Practical Guide to Claims Arising from Fatal Accidents' by James Patience
'A Practical Guide to Subtle Brain Injury Claims' by Pankaj Madan

www.ingramcontent.com/pod-product-compliance
Ingram Content Group UK Ltd.
Pitfield, Milton Keynes, MK11 3LW, UK
UKHW021240300926
15471UKWH00013B/772

9 781912 687978